UNIVERSITY OF NORTH CAROLINA
STUDIES IN COMPARATIVE LITERATURE

NUMBER 38

# UNIVERSITY OF NORTH CAROLINA
## STUDIES IN COMPARATIVE LITERATURE

*Editorial Committee*

Editor: William J. DeSua, Italian and Comparative Literature

Edwin L. Brown
Alfred G. Engstrom

O. B. Hardison

John E. Keller
Dan W. Patterson

Founded by: Werner P. Friederich, German and Comparative Literature

*For other volumes in this series see page 171.*

Foreign Sales through Librairie E. Droz, 11 Rue Massot, Geneva, Switzerland

# WORLD OF MANY LOVES:
# THE HEPTAMERON
# OF
# MARGUERITE DE NAVARRE

BY

JULES GELERNT

CHAPEL HILL
THE UNIVERSITY OF NORTH CAROLINA PRESS
1966

*Printed in the Netherlands by Royal VanGorcum Ltd., Assen*

UXORI CARISSIMAE

# PREFACE

A collection of tales modeled on the *Decameron*, Marguerite de Navarre's *Heptameron* has remained popular since its publication in the sixteenth century because it fulfills a necessary condition of popularity: it entertains its reader and gives him pleasure. Its serious purpose – to teach the new manners of polite society developed at the Italian courts – has long been recognized by scholars; what has not been seen, however, is that it reaches beyond the limitations of the courtesy-book intending to teach while entertaining.

Actually, the *Heptameron* is a *trattato d'amore*, a Renaissance treatise on love which, to be rightly understood, must be viewed in relation to the vast body of medieval and Renaissance literature of love. It must be set against a complex background comprising both the 'idealist' line that runs from courtly *fin amor* through stilnovism and Petrarchism to Florentine Neoplatonism, and the 'realist' tradition of the *fabliau* and novella that finds its finest artistic expression in Boccaccio's masterpiece. So to view it, so to set it has been my purpose in this study.

Although the point of view taken here is 'comparative,' it is still focused on a single work, and since the aim is to understand the *Heptameron*, its sources in Marguerite's life are as significant as the literary tradition in which it originates. Therefore, this study opens with a brief biographical chapter which seeks to define the woman Marguerite became as she balanced her worldly obligations with her spiritual needs. Only then, in the second chapter, do I turn to the literary tradition from which she drew her inspiration. As the elements of this tradition – be they Petrarchist, Platonist, or Ovidian – were commonplaces of Renaissance thought that could have reached her through innumerable channels, I have deliberately avoided the hunt for specific sources and analogues – a chase that strikes me as a self-defeating task. I have therefore also refrained from retracing the steps of those scholars who have wrestled with this vexing question; anyone interested in pursuing it should consult Jourda's examination of the problem in his thorough study of Marguerite's life and works.

Since Marguerite de Navarre worked within a well-defined tradition, it is her use of the highly conventional material at her disposal that should be of prime interest to the student of the *Heptameron*. I have therefore tried, in discussing the tales and the interlocutors' discussions that follow them, to define both what is conventional and what is new in her presentation of attitudes and ideas. Her originality – this is the main idea developed in the third and fourth chapters – lies in her attempt to fuse temporal and spiritual values into a livable ethics, to take an objective, realistic view of the world and infuse it with a new idealism derived not only from the clichés of courtly and romantic love but also from the teaching of the Evangelical humanists of her day. It is this which places the Queen of Navarre squarely in the stream of the broad European cultural tradition known as Christian humanism.

Lastly, a few words of acknowledgment. I wish to express my thanks to the Dean of Graduate Studies of the City University of New York, Mina Rees, for making the publication of this book financially possible. I also wish to thank Professors Maurice J. Valency and Donald M. Frame for their helpful comments on the manuscript, and voice my great debt of gratitude to my friend Marian Burkhart for her generous help in editing the text. Needless to say, its flaws are mine, and mine alone.

J.G.
*Brooklyn College*
*June 1966*

# TABLE OF CONTENTS

# CHAPTER I / SISTER OF THE KING

## PART I

When on April 11, 1492, a daughter was born to Charles d'Orléans, Count of Angoulême, and his wife, Louise de Savoie, the
brilliance of her future could hardly have been foreseen. The
Angoulême, a minor branch of the house of Orléans, were distant
cousins of the ruling house of Valois; living in straitened circumstances on an impoverished estate, they rarely came to court to be
snubbed by their royal relatives. Charles was, it is true, heir
presumptive to the throne after his cousin Louis, the influential
Duke of Orléans, but a few months after the birth of Marguerite he
saw his last hope of improving his fortunes vanish: the son then
born to Charles VIII ended the expectations of all collateral
claimants to the throne.[1]

The hopes of the family revived, however, in 1495, when the
young Dauphin died, nor were they shattered by the death of
Charles d'Orléans in 1496, for he left a son, François (born in
1494), to inherit his title and expectations. Left alone to guide
her family and its fortunes, Louise de Savoie soon found herself
embroiled in a struggle for the guardianship of her children, for
the Duke of Orléans wanted to keep an eye on the boy who was
now second in line, after himself, to the French throne. Though
Louise won the battle and was allowed to retain effective guardianship, her cousin did not admit defeat and the silent tug-of-war
between the two ended only when François finally came to the

[1] See Pierre Jourda, *Marguerite d'Angoulême, Duchesse d'Alençon, Reine de Navarre*
(Paris, 1930) I, 3-6. Unless otherwise indicated, the material for this chapter is
drawn from this exhaustive two-volume study of the life and works of the Queen
of Navarre.

throne in 1515. As long as Charles VIII lived, the Countess of Angoulême won her points; but upon his death in 1498 the Duke became King Louis XII, and this event initiated for the proud Louise de Savoie a period of bitter humiliation. Mother of the heir to the throne, she found herself not only forced into exile from her rightful place at court, where a hostile Queen could not tolerate her presence, but also required to live under the constant surveillance of an agent of the king, who had been made responsible for the education of her son. The family was, in effect, prisoner of the king, and the overriding issue that dominated the childhood of Marguerite and her brother was the ever present danger that an heir who would rob them of their prospects might be born to Louis.

Although Louise de Savoie centered her affections and ambitions so exclusively on her son that she scarcely mentioned her daughter in her diary while constantly referring to François,[2] she did not neglect the girl's education, and if Marguerite shared her brother's games and lessons, it was from her mother that she acquired her love of reading and meditation. The Countess of Angoulême loved books enough to cherish and add to the family's sizable library, and to open to her daughter its riches: Marguerite spent many an afternoon perusing its collection of romances, novellas, and treatises which were shelved alongside editions of Dante and Petrarch, Aristotle and Plato. And worried or not about the family's political future, the circle of Louise de Savoie was pleasant and relaxed, modeling its life on the cultured conviviality practiced by the polite society of the Italian courts.[3] "L'oisiveté, l'effacement

---

[2] Jourda, I, 20: "... c'est à peine si, dans son *Journal*, elle parle de sa fille, alors qu'il est sans cesse question de François d'Angoulême."

[3] Castiglione's *Cortegiano*, which at once defines and exemplifies the ideal social existence of the courtier, was, it is true, completed in 1514 and published only in 1528 (though it circulated widely in manuscript form before then). But it obviously represents a culmination of what was already established social practice: "all the antecedent history of the past two centuries had been gradually producing the conditions under which his courtier flourished; and the Italian of the Re-

politique, avaient favorisé chez les Angoulême le goût des lettres et des arts: malgré ses soucis Louise ne renonça pas aux plaisirs qu'elle avait goûtés au début de son mariage. "[4] Marguerite's formative years in such a milieu, where she could hear the sophisticated cadences and relaxed rhythms of brilliant conversationalists, provided an ideal of cultivated sociability which lay at the heart of her intellectual development and which, coupled with the beauty of the Loire valley, its distance from the intrigues and machinations of the court, made the setting of her youth – in her adult eyes – almost idyllic. Her greatest tribute to its charm is to be found in the conversations which animate the pages of the *Heptameron*.

This life came to an end for Marguerite in 1509, when she was married to Charles, Duke of Alençon, a man she neither loved nor found companionable, but who was nonetheless, in the eyes of the world, a good match for the almost dowerless young girl. Charles d'Alençon had little to recommend him personally; he was nothing but a soldier and had none of the cultural interests which were sprouting at court and among the friends of Louise de Savoie.[5] Neither attractive, intelligent, nor cultured, he did not even possess the newly fashionable surface polish of the Renaissance soldier-turned-courtier. Marguerite, it seems, felt nothing but indifference for him, rarely mentioning him in her correspondence. Buried away in Alençon, she did not have even the consolation of living with people among whom she might gratify her social and intellectual inclinations. The six years she spent separated from those she loved cannot have been happy. Fortunately, on January

---

naissance, as he appeared to the rest of Europe, was such a gentleman as he depicts." J. A. Symonds, *Renaissance in Italy: The Age of the Despots* (London, 1880) p. 168. For an account of social conversational practice prior to and during the Italian Renaissance see Thomas F. Crane, *Italian Social Customs of the Sixteenth Century and their Influence on the Literature of Europe* (New Haven, 1920) *passim*.

4 Jourda, I, 23.

5 Jourda, I, 34: "Très en retard sur son temps, il n'avait aucun des goûts qui s'éveillaient autour de Louis XII, d'Anne de Bretagne, de Louise de Savoie."

1, 1515, Louis XII died without issue, and her brother, now Francis I, hastily summoned her from her provincial exile to share with him the triumph and honors of the crown.

The accession of Francis I marked the beginning of a new era in French life, as the youthful king and his sister inaugurated that enthusiastic imitation of Italian fashions and manners which spearheaded the Renaissance in France. French aristocrats had discovered Italy when they crossed the Alps in 1494 with Charles VIII, but with the house of Angoulême the discovery bore fruit: a new generation came to the fore, fired with the exuberance of youth to emulate what it had seen in the artistic and social paradise that was Italy. During the early years of the new reign life with the king seemed a perpetual holiday as he imported artists and architects from Italy to build, expand, or adorn the many châteaux of the Loire valley to which he frequently moved his court. Pleasure was the watchword, as if the young king were deliberately throwing off the somewhat puritanical severity of the preceding reign.

While Louise de Savoie was embroiled in the daily business of government, Marguerite's function was to shine at court. And shine she did: she was warm and intelligent, the unmistakable favorite of her brother, the polished product of her background. "Elle joue," writes Jourda, "à la cour et dans notre littérature, le rôle des grandes dames d'Urbin ou de Ferrare dont elle admirait le goût exquis, l'intelligence et la sensibilité."[6] No wonder that she effaced her sickly sister-in-law, Queen Claude. After the snubs of Anne de Bretagne and the emotional isolation of Alençon, it was thrilling for the young duchess to find herself the unchallenged social queen of the realm, and the feasts and festivities at which she presided, the homage and adulation she received from ambassadors and courtiers confirmed her membership in the enchanted circle of the wielders of power. Her triumph was intoxicating and she enjoyed every moment of it.

[6] Jourda, II, 1080.

4

But Marguerite's function in the Angoulême triumvirate which now ruled France extended beyond the court and the salon. She represented the king in the provinces, marshalled troops, supervised the construction of fortifications, and received ambassadors. Her brother sought her advice, knowing her to be a devoted and trustworthy adjunct. And she always had access to him — a fact well known throughout Europe: if one wished to reach the king, one approached Marguerite. Yet Pierre Jourda, in his study of the Queen of Navarre, concludes that despite the adulation bestowed upon her from far and wide, despite her diplomatic activity, hers was never more than a secondary political role. She had no voice in the making of policy, and she herself was well aware of the limitations set upon her political functions when she described herself as a second pair of eyes and ears for the king. Although she may at times have influenced her brother's decisions, she primarily implemented them, and in this capacity her usefulness was incalculable.

This political and administrative activity began in 1524 when François, moving to defend Provence against the invading Imperial army of Charles V, pursued the invaders into Italy. Louise de Savoie was named regent and Marguerite shared the burden of administering the realm. On February 24 of the following year the French forces suffered a disastrous defeat at the battle of Pavia; a week later a stunned court learned the news of the king's capture and his brother-in-law's flight from battle.

Marguerite's anxiety for her brother's welfare was intense, but she felt equally concerned for her husband out of a strong sense of loyalty. She even felt compassion for the sick, despairing man who returned from the battle with his soldier's reputation tarnished, and set about to nurse him through his illness with all the devotion she could command. Her efforts were to no avail. Charles d'Alençon died on April 11, 1525, leaving her deeply moved even though their life together in the fifteen years of their marriage had been barely affectionate. But there was no time for personal grief: the integrity of the crown had to be preserved

5

against the attempted encroachments of a mutinous nobility, a rebellious merchant class, and defiant *parlements*, all of whom sought to promote their independence of the crown in the absence of the king. His return soon became imperative, and in August Marguerite was on her way to Spain to negotiate his release. There she nursed her ailing brother and dickered fruitlessly with the representatives of the Emperor: Charles V demanded Burgundy in exchange for the king and would hear of no ransom. Her unsuccessful mission nevertheless brought badly needed moral support to François and paved the way for the subsequent Treaty of Madrid (1526), which set him free. Consequently, when Marguerite returned to France in December 1525, the court accorded her a heroine's welcome. She had reached the zenith of her glory.[7]

In 1527 she celebrated her marriage to Henri d'Albret, King of Navarre; this wedding was a love match – at least for Marguerite. She has left us a picture of their relationship in the *Heptameron*, where he appears as Hircan, the proud aristocrat, handsome and attractive, who respects and admires the social grace and mental abilities of his wife, the sagacious Parlamente, even while he insists on his masculine prerogative to be unfaithful to his heart's content. Though Marguerite was hurt by her husband's numerous infidelities, this marriage at least was not the empty shell the first one had been. And in 1528 one of her deepest desires was fulfilled when she gave birth to her first child, Jeanne, the only one of her children to live past infancy.

Political affairs still took up most of her time. In 1529 she accompanied her mother to Cambrai, where they met with Margaret of Austria, aunt of Charles V, to discuss the cessation of hostilities which had resumed after the king's return to France. The *Paix des Dames*, as the treaty they negotiated came to be called, set the terms for the release of his children, who had been held as hostages in Madrid under the terms of the treaty of 1526. But for

[7] On Marguerite's mission to Spain, see Jourda, I, 108-136.

the first time in her adult life her concerns became more important to her than her brother's. She was queen of Navarre, yet the greater part of her kingdom was in the hands of Charles V, and with her husband she dreamed of regaining the lost territories. That François' policies did not accord with Henri d'Albret's ambitions caused her considerable pain, for she was intensely loyal to both, and the machinations the situation called forth were not pretty. The king of Navarre, knowing that he had little to hope for from his brother-in-law, tried to achieve his ends by approaching the Emperor and playing him against the French king. But Charles V was too shrewd to fall into the trap; besides, he knew that France would not support an attack on Spanish Navarre since François, more interested in Milan than in Navarre,[8] had secretly pledged not to give aid to Henri d'Albret. With no effective bargaining position, Henri's double-dealing game with king and emperor served only to arouse his brother-in-law's suspicions. Marguerite, as a party to at least some of these maneuvers, fell under her brother's displeasure as well.

The 1530's presented other problems too. As early as 1521 Marguerite had become interested in the work of a group of reformers who wished to cleanse the Church of abuses without breaking with it, and before the disaster of Pavia she had tried to win her mother and brother to the cause.[9] Louise de Savoie, a sincerely religious woman, had been interested, but her son's concern was purely political. The ensuing military campaigns and their aftermath ruled out the possibility of serious action in this area on the part of the crown. Yet the religious controversy did not abate: the Reformation was making rapid progress in France,

---

[8] "Marguerite, en 1531, reprochait à son frère et à sa mère de penser au Milanais plus qu'à la Navarre." Jourda, I, 224.
[9] This group, known as *le groupe de Meaux*, was led by Briçonnet, bishop of Meaux, and included, among others, Lefèvre d'Etaples, Michel d'Arande, and Gérard Roussel. For Marguerite's relations with Briçonnet, see Jourda, I, 66-92, 95-99; also P. A. Becker, *Marguerite, duchesse d'Angoulême, et Guillaume Briçonnet, évêque de Meaux, d'après leur correspondance manuscrite, 1521-1524* (Paris, 1901).

thereby stiffening the resistance of the ultra-orthodox party led by the Sorbonne and making the position of the moderates – among them Louise de Savoie and the king – increasingly difficult to maintain.

When Louise died in 1531, François was left to deal with an explosive situation all by himself, since Marguerite was too deeply committed to the reform party to be useful as a moderator. And the explosion came two years later when she invited Gérard Roussel, a member of this group of reformers, to preach at the Louvre during Lent of 1533. The Sorbonne was up in arms: it knew that Marguerite was responsible for Roussel's presence at court and felt sufficiently strong to attack the king's sister in a formal condemnation for heresy of her *Miroir de l'âme pécheresse*, which had been published in 1531. The king forced the Sorbonne to retract its verdict, but the following year the *affaire des placards*, touched off by the posting of an attack against the Mass all over Paris and even on the king's bedroom door, aroused such strong passions that François was forced to take effective measures against the reformers. Marguerite, for her part, found it wiser to leave court and retire to her estates in the south, where many advocates of religious reform took refuge with her.[10] François was very fond of his sister; nonetheless, her involvement in the controversy coupled with her husband's politicking must have made him very glad to see her go.

Relations between brother and sister reached their lowest point over the issue of Jeanne d'Albret's marriage. In the king's eyes children were potentially useful political property and had to be carefully watched, just as he himself had been securely guarded during his childhood. In 1538, disturbed by his brother-in-law's flirtation with Spain, he ordered Jeanne to the château of Plessis-lez-Tours where she became virtually his prisoner. Two years later the Duke of Cleves defected from the Imperial alliance and sought the support of France, and François conceived the project of

[10] On Marguerite's activities in connection with Church reform, see Jourda, I, 140-142, 169-197.

marrying his niece to the duke in order to cement the new alignment. At the same time, in order to obtain Henri d'Albret's consent to the marriage, he proposed a plan of attack designed to reconquer Spanish Navarre. Henri agreed enthusiastically at first, but when he realized that François would never go to war for the interests of Navarre, he changed his mind. As for Marguerite, she had strong reservations from the very start; she had hoped for a more brilliant match for her daughter and was as well deeply offended by her brother's arbitrariness in dealing with the girl. Jeanne, too, opposed the marriage; in a stormy interview with her uncle she maintained her opposition to the very last, and literally had to be whipped into obedience on her mother's orders! The king insisted, and a heart-broken Marguerite saw her daughter married to the Duke of Cleves on June 14, 1541.

As Jeanne was not yet thirteen, the marriage was not consummated, and the only concession won by her parents was that she be allowed to remain in France instead of following her husband to Cleves. There was no further talk of the expedition into Spain, and while Jeanne, exhausted by the tensions of the preceding weeks, lay ill at Plessis-lez-Tours, Marguerite had to follow her brother to Lyon, for he, still drawn by Milan, wanted to keep an eye on the Emperor.

After her daughter's marriage Marguerite regained François' confidence, and even his discovery of Henri d'Albret's plot to open the southern border to Charles V's armies – a proposal of which Marguerite was totally ignorant – did not diminish his trust in his sister. Yet despite the renewal of kingly favor, Marguerite realized she had nothing further to expect from her brother. He had destroyed her hopes for her daughter and for Navarre, and her credit at court would never be more than shaky. In the fall of 1542, therefore, she joined her husband, who was keeping watch over the border of Biscay.

This self-imposed exile was to give the Queen her first taste of life in her own realm. Whenever she could get away from the business of government, she would retire to one of her châteaux

– Nérac, Pau, and Mont-de-Marsan were her favorites – to enjoy the pleasures of country life. Prayer, meditation, reading, and walks through the countryside – these were her activities as the days flowed in even succession. News from court, the arrival of a new book were events in this retirement, topics for the conversational art of the little circle of friends and retainers she had gathered about her.

> On consacrait à Dieu les premières heures de la matinée, puis Marguerite en 'simple habit' groupait autour d'elle ses officiers et ses dames, et l'on devisait, durant des heures, tout en travaillant, des affaires du jour, des nouvelles venues de France.... La conversation allait sans guide, librement, sans contrainte, rebondissant sur un mot, prenant les chemins les plus variés. Les nouvelles épuisées, quelqu'un soulevait un problème de morale ou d'histoire, contait une anecdote qui donnait à la discussion une direction nouvelle; les humanistes, les poètes lisaient leurs vers: la Reine, parfois, à l'appui de ses avis, égrenait ses souvenirs..., chacun développait son point de vue, défendait ses théories....[11]

Anyone familiar with the *Heptameron* will recognize the scene. It was probably during these peaceful days that Marguerite conceived the idea of the book and began working on it.

Unlike the narrators of the *Heptameron*, however, Marguerite and her friends were not isolated from the surrounding world. She kept abreast of the international situation. Thus, according to Paget, the English ambassador, she was one of the very few to know of the secret negotiations being conducted between England and France. She pushed for an alliance between the two countries, since she feared a rapprochement with Charles V that would definitively rule out any hope of recovering Navarre's Spanish territories. But she need not have feared; the war with Spain was resumed. One consequence was that her daughter's much detested marriage was dissolved; for, after suffering a crushing defeat at the hands of the Emperor, the Duke of Cleves was forced to renounce

[11] Jourda, I, 294.

the alliance with France, and Marguerite seized the opportunity to obtain an annullment for Jeanne.[12]

In the meantime her brother once again pressed her into service. Since Henri d'Albret was in Paris, she was put in charge of the southern province of Guyenne to prepare against an enemy attack, a task which kept her occupied for more than a year and a half, so that it was only in the spring of 1544 that she was able to rejoin the king. By then France's situation had become critical: the Imperial armies had overrun the North, had entered Champagne, and threatened Paris itself. The king, ill and exhausted, kept his sister at his side, seeing only her and two other close associates. While Parisians were near panic and ruin threatened the whole country, she attended calmly to business – she even found time to sign papers putting into effect regulations for the hospital of Argentan – and worked for a negotiated peace by sending her confessor to confer with the confessor of Charles V, thus initiating the preliminary contacts which led eventually to the signing of the Treaty of Crépy in October, 1544. Needless to say, the peace terms ignored the interests of Navarre.

After the cessation of hostilities Marguerite returned to Navarre with her husband. She was weary of politics and took no further part in her husband's intrigues; instead, she devoted herself to the administration of her lands. In March, 1547, came the shock of her brother's death; her intense sorrow kept her cloistered in the monastery of Tusson for several weeks before she felt able to face a world of new concerns. That the new king, Henri II, did not like her she knew, and she wondered if he would continue to pay the pension her brother had granted her – an important question since it constituted a large part of her income. Though Henri did not suspend the pension, he delivered a far more painful blow in ordering Jeanne to marry Antoine de Bourbon, Duke of Vendôme.

12 Jourda, I, 282. The annullment was finally granted by Pope Paul III on November 15, 1545. Cf. Pierre Jourda, *Répertoire analytique et chronologique de la correspondance de Marguerite d'Angouléme, Duchesse d'Alençon, Reine de Navarre (1492-1549)* (Paris, 1930) Nos. 998, 1000, and 1001.

11

Her hopes of a brilliant marriage for her daughter once again dashed, Marguerite, exhausted, retired to Navarre immediately after the nuptials, leaving a husband who had grown indifferent to her, a king who only mocked her, and a daughter who showed no regret at her departure.

Jeanne had never responded to her mother's somewhat overwhelming affection and, furthermore, eagerly desired this marriage. Supremely happy with her husband, the new bride could hardly sympathize with her mother's sorrow over the match. And yet, her daughter was to give Marguerite her last happy moments. From March to May 1549 Jeanne and her husband visited the Queen, and the sight of her daughter's happiness renewed Marguerite's interest in life. When they left, she was once again alone. In poor health since the death of her brother, she knew her own end was not far off. She fell ill in December and, lingering for some twenty days, awaited the death that finally came on the twenty-first.[13]

A true princess of the Renaissance, Marguerite had energy for amazingly varied activities. In spite of her political and administrative duties, she found time for the reformation of convents and monasteries,[14] the founding of hospitals, the encouragement of artists, writers, and scholars. She sponsored translations, fostered the dissemination of new ideas, and whenever possible intervened when the safety of her protégés was threatened by the Sorbonne.[15] One may well wonder why a royal princess, queen in her own right, for many years the undisputed ruler of fashionable society, should in the midst of such an active life feel the need to engage in a literary career that would expose her secure reputation to the uncertainties of literary judgment.

[13] Jourda, I, 339; see also note 102.
[14] In reference to Marguerite's interest in reforming convents, cf. Jourda, Répertoire, Nos. 23, 481, 514, and 552.
[15] On Marguerite's relations with reformers, see Jourda, I, 69-78, 173-182, 184-189, 212, 306-307. Cf. also Jourda, Répertoire, passim.

## PART II

Beside the brilliant princess there was in Marguerite de Navarre a profoundly religious woman who yearned for spiritual illumination, a woman who craved to give and receive love. It is that woman who found in writing a means of self-expression, who in her literary works voiced and answered the emotional and spiritual needs that her worldly career did not satisfy. Her writings are in great measure spiritual autobiography, the record of her experience of life. A proper understanding of the *Heptameron* therefore requires that we become as aware of the Queen of Navarre's spiritual life as of the literary context within which she wrote.

Marguerite's character was marked by her need to love and be loved[16] — a need which must have developed early in life, for Louise de Savoie so concentrated her affection on her son that little was left for her daughter. At any rate, Marguerite also centered her love on François, and despite his selfishness, despite the pain he inflicted on her in later life, her love never faltered. Her brother was so used to being the cynosure of the household that he never appreciated her need for affection and took from her far more than he ever gave. For her part she was too much governed by the attitudes of her time to resent his position consciously; besides, since the family's hopes all rested on him, it would seem only natural that François be the center of attention. Yet the frustration was undoubtedly real, if unackowledged, and while she might have expected to find fulfillment in marriage, there, too, she met with disappointment. Charles d'Alençon gave her neither companionship nor children; and what is worse, the flighty, pleasure-seeking Henri d'Albret, whom she loved, soon tired of her and turned to other women.[17]

---

[16] Cf. Jourda, I, 67: "Ce besoin d'aimer, qui est la marque de son caractère, ce désir de se sentir entourée de sympathies...."
[17] Loyal as she was, Marguerite could not resist commenting on Henri's behavior in letters to Montmorency, her brother's right-hand man: "... vous priant que quand le roy de Navarre sera auprès de vous... vous le consillés en tout ce

Even in her role as mother Marguerite found more pain than pleasure. She had hoped vainly for a child during her first marriage; in her second she had several miscarriages and lost her son, Jean (born on July 15, 1530), in infancy. Jeanne, a cold, undemonstrative child, was buffeted about as a pawn of the French king, separated from her mother, forced into a marriage against her will; only after her happy marriage to Antoine de Bourbon did she feel free to return a measure of her mother's doting affection.[18]

Neither as child, sister, wife, nor mother, then, did Marguerite ever receive in any way what she gave to others, and no amount of social success could compensate for the emotional void she endured. That she should turn for solace to the love which permeates the Christian mystery is understandable. "Elle avait connu la gloire du monde," writes a recent commentator, "elle n'avait jamais connu l'amour. La religion qu'elle se fit la montre insatis-

qu'il aura à faire, comme luy et moy avons en vous nostre vraye fiance; et puisque vous y estes, je n'ay point de peur que tout n'aille bien, sinon que vous ne le puissiés garder d'aimer les dames espaignoles...." *Lettres de Marguerite d'Angoulême*, F. Génin, ed. (Paris, 1841) No. 73, p. 246 (No. 457 in Jourda, *Répertoire*). If the above sounds light-hearted, there is no mistaking the bitterness behind the following: "Mon nepveu, j'ay receu les lettres que m'avez escriptes, par lesquelles j'ay congneu que vous estes trop meilleur parent que le roy de Navarre n'est bon mary, car vous seul m'avez faict sçavoir des nouvelles du Roy et de luy, sans qu'il ait voulu donner le plaisir à une pouvre femme grosse de luy escripre ung seul mot. Je remets à vostre bon jugement s'il a faict le debvoir qui apartient en cest endroit." *Ibid.*, No. 76, p. 248 (No. 505 in *Répertoire*). Cf. the following as well: "J'entends bien que si vous voulez croire le roy de Navarre, qu'il vous fera faire tant de désordre qu'il vous gastera...," *ibid.*, No. 78, p. 251 (No. 463 in *Répertoire*).
[18] Not only was Jeanne forced into her first marriage with her mother's consent – albeit reluctant consent, but Marguerite strenuously opposed her much-desired second marriage. Henri II, a few days after the ceremony, wrote to Montmorency and the Duke of Aumale that "la reine de Navarre est le plus mal qu'il est possible avec son mary pour l'amour de sa fille laquelle ne tient compte de sa mère. Vous ne vistes jamais tant pleurer que a faict ma tante au partir, et si il n'eust esté de moy, elle ne fut jamais retournée avec son mary." Letter of October 24, 1548, quoted in Comte H. de La Ferrière-Percy, *Marguerite d'Angoulême, son livre de dépenses (1540-1549)* (Paris, 1862) pp. 128-129.

faite de ce qu'elle eut, et cherchant à se payer de ce qui lui manqua."[19]

Marguerite's highly personal religious convictions evolved as a result of the absence of real satisfaction in her spiritual life. Her soul, she writes in the *Miroir de l'âme pécheresse*, was given over to the pleasures of the world; self-love had extinguished the light of God in her; the formalities of worship were nothing more than a boring habit; and she was, she says, lost and confused:

> Moy, qui estois de vous tant séparée,
> Et en mon coeur et mon sens esgarée....[20]

Her bewilderment, heightened as it was by her concern over the outcome of the struggle with Spain, led her to search for a more durable, more rewarding meaning to life than that offered by the glitter and intoxication of a brilliant career at court. In 1521 she engaged in correspondence with Briçonnet, bishop of Meaux and nominal leader of the group of reformers named after his city. These men sought to apply the new learning of humanist scholarship to the study of Scripture in order to clarify the essentially spiritual meaning of the Christian faith. They were not Protestants; as already noted, they sought only to reform the Church from within, to stress the spirit rather than the letter of Christian doctrine without breaking with the fundamental dogma of Catholicism. Marguerite, in sympathy with their program, exchanged letters with Briçonnet for four years, seeking spiritual guidance and receiving from the prelate advice, interpretations of Biblical texts, and exhortations to win the king and his mother to the cause of reform.

The correspondence came to an end in 1524, probably because Marguerite had outgrown her need for the hazily mystical ministrations that came to her from Meaux. Nonetheless, Bri-

[19] Verdun L. Saulnier, ed., 'Introduction,' in Marguerite de Navarre, *Théâtre Profane* (Paris, 1946) p. xii.
[20] Marguerite de Navarre, *Le Miroir de l'âme pécheresse*, in *Les Marguerites de la Marguerite des princesses*, F. Frank, ed. (Paris, 1873) I, 41.

çonnet's influence was profound. He encouraged her predilection for a religion of feeling rather than of intellect, and it is he who put her in the habit of bringing everything back to God, leading her to a mystique which, stripped of its symbolic terminology, comes down to an appreciation of love and an indulgence in dreamy speculation.

Marguerite absorbed the nourishment provided by her spiritual mentor and derived comfort and moral support from it; she had yet to assimilate it. Briçonnet's exhortation that she die to the world in order to live more ardently in her heart and spirit did indeed appeal to her idealistic nature, yet at heart she was not one to reject the world. For alongside the troubled woman athirst for spiritual illumination, there was in her a worldly-wise princess who, making the best of her contemporaries' mores, could even become a party to them. Her problem was to find a way of coming to terms with the world, and the mysticism of a Briçonnet provided her with only one of the clues to the many-faceted riddle of life. One critic has described her as a conscience in a continuous state of crisis,[21] and it is tempting to dramatize her life by portraying a Marguerite engaged in a heroic struggle to free herself from worldly attachments. But such a picture would be far from the truth. The conflict of allegiance between God and Caesar is at least as old as Christianity itself, and Marguerite could not avoid facing it; but hers was a search for unity, and her intellectual activity was devoted to the formulation of a reasonable, livable synthesis of spiritual and earthly values.

She did not reject life; rather, like the Dante she admired so much, she sought to bring it into harmony with the divine principle which she believed was its source and animation, and her whole literary career was, I believe, an attempt to achieve this end. Writing provided her with the opportunity to give expression to her feelings, and at the same time forced her to organize these

[21] "Et surtout une Marguerite, conscience toujours en crise, et dont le cœur secret – une fois 'embarquée,' eût dit Pascal – ne sait pas aborder, et ne touchera plus terre." Saulnier, in *Théâtre profane*, p. xvii.

feelings as well as her thoughts into some sort of coherent order. In short, it led to self-discovery, and if, as Jourda states categorically, it was around 1520 that she wrote her first poems,[22] then we may rightly associate her literary activity with her search for values.

Jourda suggests, quite perceptively it seems to me, that Marguerite's career as a poet was launched under the influence of Briçonnet: by encouraging her bent for meditation, by urging her to read and study the Bible, he brought her to the point where, one day, quite naturally, she turned to verse for the expression of her spiritual misgivings and her love for the members of her family. Poetry to her was natural, perhaps, because she knew and loved the literature of the past. In the *Roman de la rose* she came upon an idealistic dream of love subsequently debunked by the ironic realism of its second part; in Petrarch she followed the struggle between a man's desire for fame and his awareness of an eternal divinity that reduces worldliness to nought; in Boccaccio she witnessed the conflict between man's sensuality and his spiritual being. Were not these the very issues that disturbed her so profoundly and led her to seek the counsel of her friend the bishop of Meaux? Certainly she was aware of the gap separating human practice from Christian ideals, and she surely must have felt the contradiction between the commands of divine law and the practical demands of human necessity. Through the medium of poetry she could perhaps discover and then express her sense of a reality which would encompass both sets of truths – a vision of life solidly anchored in the reality of human experience, yet reaching for the divine essence which permeates all existence.

Marguerite's works are thus characterized as much by her interest in man's mode of living as by her concern for his ultimate destination. If she gave religious questions a dominant place, it is because the orthodox solutions had calcified and provided no satisfactory answers for the thinking men of the sixteenth century.

[22] Jourda, I, 99.

God, it was felt, had become the toy of a decadent scholasticism which had so choked the spirit of religious faith that it had reduced Christianity to a monstrously oppressive carcass of meaningless ritual, while the life of the spirit had been debased by the worldly hypocrisy of a complacent clergy – a clergy whose practices Marguerite attacked more than once in the *Heptameron*. Hence the Queen's interest in religion was part of her personal search for values – not just rules – to live by, and to make it the exclusive concern of her life is to misconstrue her nature. Neither a theologian nor a philosopher, but a moralist deeply concerned with human experience, she confined her vision to the limits of her heart.[23]

The essence of Marguerite's thought on the religious questions of the day – in other words, her appraisal of the enduring values that men might live by – is perhaps most clearly set into relief by her late play, the *Comédie de Mont-de Marsan* (1548).[24] For the objective

---

[23] Cf. the following comment: "La théologie de Marguerite se ramène à la Bible et particulièrement à saint Paul; simplifiée, réduite à une très pure essence de christianisme évangélique et paulinien, elle émeut le sentiment plus qu'elle ne satisfait le besoin de connaître." A. Renaudet, "Marguerite de Navarre, à propos d'un ouvrage récent," *Revue du XVIe Siècle*, XVIII (1931) 305.

[24] A full-length study of Marguerite de Navarre's religion has yet to be written. Here it may be sufficient to point out that she was not a systematic thinker who could submit to the shackles of a rigorously conceived doctrine, but rather an eclectic who chose at the moment whatever fulfilled the need of the moment. Hence the disagreement among scholars about the nature of her religious beliefs. Lefranc, in his Introduction to the *Dernières poésies* (Paris, 1896), will have her a Protestant; yet the occasional correspondence of her ideas to those of Luther or Calvin (e.g. the *Miroir de l'âme pécheresse*) is due far more to an affinity of feeling than to doctrinal conviction. Jourda (I, 605), basing himself on the play under discussion, argues for mystic quietism as the solution Marguerite found on the eve of her death (for that matter, he might also have adduced the elevated, 'mystic' tone of Marguerite's correspondence with Vittoria Colonna, a sample of which may be found in E. Picot, *Les Français italianisants au XVIe siècle* [Paris, 1906] I, 45, and which he summarizes in I, 247-249). For his part, Lucien Febvre, in *Autour de l'Heptaméron: amour sacré, amour profane* (Paris 1944), seems unable to come to a definite conclusion, although he appears to favor a Lutheran Marguerite.

nature of the dramatic medium forced Marguerite to define disparate points of view and thus avoid the haziness which her attempts at reconciling them led to in her meditative poems. In the dialogues she assigned each point of view to a separate character, and the interchange of ideas provides both definition and synthesis. Set upon the stage are characters with decided opinions who are forced to explain themselves by the very shock of their contact with one another, and if Marguerite's style borders on confession, it is because these characters are really herself. But that is the very reason why such a late play affords a clear view of the issues that engrossed her mind.

The *Comédie de Mont-de-Marsan* introduces four women – La Mondaine, La Superstitieuse, La Sage, and La Ravie de l'Amour de Dieu – who represent four points of view on the goals of life and

The most useful discussion of the question to date may be found in the introductions Saulnier has written for his edition of Marguerite's *Théâtre profane*.

Actually, Marguerite's religious position was not an isolated phenomenon in her century. Together with such writers as Rabelais, Marot, and Des Périers, she shared and propagated the ideas of the humanist evangelism formulated by Colet, Erasmus, Lefèvre d'Etaples, and their disciples, an evangelism which sought to restore to Christianity the revivifying spirit to be found in the Bible behind the letter of the law. For a detailed study of religious positions and controversies in France at the turn of the sixteenth century, see A. Renaudet, *Préréforme et humanisme à Paris pendant les premières guerres d'Italie (1494-1517)* (Paris, 1953). Equally informative is Lucien Febvre's *Le Problème de l'incroyance au XVIe siècle* (Paris, 1942), in which, using Rabelais as illustration, the author demonstrates the existence of a strong Erasmian current among the French humanists of the earlier sixteenth century. C.-A. Mayer's *La Religion de Marot* (Genève, 1960) and M. A. Screech's *The Rabelaisian Marriage* (London, 1958), though more limited in scope, also help define the nature of evangelical humanism.

As for Marguerite herself, it is to Lefèvre d'Etaples, whose doctrine reached her through the ministrations of Briçonnet, that we must refer in order to understand her basic religious orientation. Fabrism was marked by the desire to concentrate all of Christian doctrine into the dogmas of grace and redemption (Renaudet, *Préréforme*, p. 631); these are the very themes that dominate in Marguerite's religious writings.

the means of achieving salvation.[25] La Mondaine voices the materialism of an amoral courtly society, La Superstitieuse religious bigotry, La Sage enlightened faith, and La Ravie the mysticism of direct union with God through love.[26] Four positions rather than four characters, and the play would be no more than a dull debate if not for the occasional touches of psychological observation introduced by Marguerite.

La Mondaine lives for pleasure. She loves only herself and founds her being in the tangible; as she can neither see nor touch her soul, she takes no interest in it and reserves her concern for her body and its welfare, the only realities she knows. She is the 'amie de cour' satirized by La Borderie,[27] the court lady who appears more than once in the stories of the *Heptameron*; not only does she make a fetish of her beauty, but she also knows the value of money in this world.[28] When La Superstitieuse faces her with the fact of death to demonstrate the short-sightedness of her materialism, her reply is classic – she will enjoy herself as much as she can while she lives:

[25] The most recent edition of the text, together with a most useful introduction, will be found in *Théâtre profane*, pp. 241 ff.

[26] *Théâtre profane*, p. 242.

[27] La Borderie published his attack on the materialistic court lady, *L'Amye de court*, in 1541. "L'Amye de Court est une femme qui a décidé de se passer d'idéals et qui, gagnée par le matérialisme de son siècle, veut profiter de l'ascendant que sa beauté et son rang lui donnent sur les hommes qu'elle connaît trop bien; elle sait ce qu'il faut attendre d'eux et de la vie." Emile V. Telle, *L'Oeuvre de Marguerite d'Angoulême, Reine de Navarre, et la Querelle des Femmes* (Toulouse, 1937) p. 159. Interestingly enough, it was Book III of Castiglione's *Cortegiano*, translated into French in 1537, which unleashed the "Querelle des Amyes." See Antoine Héroet, *Oeuvres poétiques*, F. Gohin, ed. (Paris, 1909), pp. xx-xxiv.

[28] La Sage:          Vous estimez donc bien peu l'or.
La Bergere:      Aultant qu'il vault, ne plus ne moins.
La Mondaine:   Vous n'en tenez guere an voz mains:
                       Parquoy ne savez ce qu'il vault. (768-771)
'La Bergere' is La Ravie, who is introduced (Scene IV) as "La Ravie de l'Amour de Dieu, Bergere" (*Théâtre profane*, p. 299).

20

Puis que ainsy est que demain je mourray,
A belle bride abatue je courray
A tout plaisir, dourmir, manger et boire;
Et passeray mon temps sy plaisamment,
Que j'auray eu parfaict contentement
Avant le jour de la dame tant noire. (149-154)

But her worldly self-centeredness ("Bref, je n'ayme rien que moy mesme" – l. 254) has its positive side. She is more curious and open-minded than the others. She converts to the doctrine of La Sage more readily than her superstitious sister, and when La Ravie's love songs dismay the others, she can approach and communicate with her. She clearly represents the worldly side of Marguerite, the mundane wisdom reflected in the creation of such characters as Saffredent, Simontault, and Nomerfide in the *Heptameron*.

La Superstitieuse, on the other hand, lives only to mortify the flesh, convinced that only through penance, through her faith in ritual and religious relics, can she save her soul. She is horrified by La Mondaine and punctuates La Sage's lecture to the pleasure-loving woman with exclamations of smug self-approval. Anti-worldly rather than otherworldly, she sees religion as magic, and, terribly proud of her ostentatious piety, she makes it her business to reform everyone else under the pretext of 'charity.' While she represents the narrow orthodoxy of the Sorbonne, she, like the Mondaine, is also drawn from real life: the type of 'grande dévote' was not unknown to Marguerite, who could find examples of it even at court, and, in the *Dialogue en forme de vision nocturne*, an early poem, accused herself of having been such a Pharisee. La Superstitieuse gets her comeuppance when La Sage condemns her ignorant self-righteousness, and it takes a good while before she is led from her blind adherence to the letter of the law to the enlightened spiritual doctrine preached by the wise lady.

La Sage's doctrine is based on a reasonable harmony between the physical and spiritual which, together, constitute man. Neither fear nor pleasure must be his guide; he is a rational being, and

21

reason will lead him to virtue both in his relationship to God and his commerce with mankind:

> L'homme raisonnable
> Est faict agréable
> A Dieu et au monde.... (171-173)

The body, being the envelope of the soul, is not to be neglected, but to be used under the guidance of reason (288 ff.). Conversely, the soul alone does not constitute the whole man, and if the soulless body is deprived of spiritual life, the disembodied soul can do no good in this world – and it is in *this* world that man lives:

> ... l'ame tant seullement
> N'est l'homme; mais l'assemblement
> Des deux, hommes lon doibt nommer.
> Corps sans ames sont cadavers,
> Charongnes pour nourrir les vers,
> Qui de l'homme n'ont nul effect;
> L'ame sans corps ne peult veoir
> Et des euvres pert le pouvoir,
> Dont elle n'est l'homme parfaict:
> Mais l'ame au corps joincte et unie,
> C'est l'homme: en ceste compaignie
> De parfaicte confaction
> Ceste union apporte vie:
> Mais si l'ame est du corps ravie,
> C'est mort leur separation. (312-326)

The soul's enlightenment comes in the reading of the Bible, and good works stem from love. Love and faith under the guidance of a reasoned understanding of the Bible – these are the requisites for the good life:

> Car, si vostre cueur n'est joieulx
> Et charitable et amoureux,
> A Dieu ne faictes que mentir....
> ... Je vous dis qu'il vous fault aller
> Le chemin des commandemens,
> Et faire bien sans vous lasser,
> Et de prier ne vous passer,
> Rememorant ses Testamens. (450-452; 484-488)

When she concludes, La Sage hands each of the ladies a copy of the Old and New Testaments; now that they have seen the light, they can find their way through life without outside help. La Sage stands apparently for the mature Marguerite; her common sense and her insistence on love as the dominant principle of human existence recall the Queen's spokesman in the *Heptameron*, Parlamente, who evidently enunciates the conclusions reached by Marguerite herself.

The question would seem to be settled, but suddenly a shepherdess, La Ravie, walks across the stage singing of her ecstatic passion for some mysterious lover. The three ladies are properly dismayed, and interestingly enough it is La Sage who is most disapproving. Passionate rapture shocks her rationality; she taxes the shepherdess with madness, and then confines herself to making impersonal comments on the conversation that ensues among the other three. La Mondaine and La Superstitieuse are confused; mistaking the shepherdess' passion for courtly love, since she uses its terminology, they try to convert her to the faith they have just embraced. But all in vain. Indifferent to the body – she is insensitive to hunger, thirst, cold, and heat, indifferent to the need for work – she is content to sing while keeping her sheep and cares nothing for the charge of idleness leveled against her, she is deaf to the call of reason. She knows nothing but love and seeks to know nothing else; she will not read even the Bible, for the path of learning is not for her – all her knowledge, she declares, consists in loving:

> Je ne sçay rien sinon aimer.
> Ce sçavoir là est mon estude,
> C'est mon chemin, sans lacitude
> Où je courray tant que je vive. (820-823)

Furthermore, she has no comprehension of the nature of her love; she merely feels it, and that suffices her. This state of constant delight abolishes all hopes and fears. She has abandoned 'reason' and 'honor' for the intoxication of her 'très douce tromperie,' which will lead her beyond her one fear of not loving enough to the point at which divine grace will descend upon her, and all will be peace within her. The ladies finally give up as the shepherdess resumes her song of love and goes on her way, completely by-passing the doctrine so carefully expounded by the enlightened wisdom of La Sage.

There are, then, two debates in this play; worldly and doctrinal blindness are opposed to enlightened wisdom, which, in turn, is shocked by the non-rational self-surrender of mysticism. The first debate reaches a resolution when wisdom teaches the other two to use their gifts well, but the gap which separates La Sage from the shepherdess is never bridged. No conclusion is possible because the Sage and Ravie represent Marguerite's own polarity. If La Sage is the walking embodiment of the moderate doctrine developed by Briçonnet and his group, then La Ravie brings to life yet one more significant influence on Marguerite's spiritual vision: that of the *libertins spirituels*.[29]

In her middle years, in the *Miroir de l'âme pécheresse*, Marguerite had voiced and experimented with a mood of abject despondency usually associated with the spirit of the Reformation: the soul, wallowing in its baseness and helplessness, more contemptible than a worm, imprisoned in the darkness of the earth, bound by its lusts, unable even to cry for help because powerless to do so, must depend for its salvation solely on the grace of God as transmitted to man through the agency of Christ. In a later work, *Les Prisons*, which like the *Comédie de Mont-de-Marsan* is contemporaneous with

---

[29] Pocque and Quintin, the leaders of the sect, taught that there were three stages in the history of religion, corresponding to the three persons of the Trinity: formal adherence to the law of the Old Testament (Father), the harmony between faith and works proclaimed in the New Testament (Son), and the innocence of pure love posited by libertinism (Holy Spirit). They further taught that each Christian undergoes a shortened form of this general evolution as he moves toward true faith. Applying these notions to Marguerite's play, some critics say that the three stages are represented by La Superstitieuse, La Sage, and La Ravie respectively, while La Mondaine stands for the pre-Christian stage of idolatry. See *Théâtre profane*, pp. 258-261.

the writing of the *Heptameron*, the dark pessimism of the *Miroir* was replaced by the positive, hopeful elements of Fabrist doctrine.[30] Marguerite still insists that only divine grace can effectively save and that justification is by faith, but when she adds that love – i.e., desire, is the impulse which leads to salvation, she has parted company not only with Calvin and his doctrine of predestination, but also with Luther and his exacting dogma of justification by faith.[31] When Marguerite suggests that man *can* hope to rise on the strength of his desire, and when she further asserts her conviction that while the illumination man needs for wisdom is miraculous it is available to those who search for it actively because it is present in the Bible, she has based her doctrine on Lefèvre's principle that "Dieu veut que tous soient sauvés et il donne sa grâce à tous. Cependant tous ne sont pas attirés par lui, il n'y a que ceux qui ne résistent pas à sa grâce."[32] That is, essentially, the doctrine of La Sage.

La Ravie, on the other hand, embodies the libertinist doctrines of inertia, innocence, and indifference to evil. According to the first, knowledge is as superfluous as works for those who let themselves be possessed by the spirit, for love reduces *scientia* and practice to nought. The second maintains that once man is

[30] *Les Prisons*, in Marguerite de Navarre, *Dernières poésies*, Abel Lefranc, ed. (Paris, 1896). The work is a long allegorical poem in three books depicting the soul's progress from mundane attachments to awareness and understanding of God through the all-important agency of the Bible. Addressed by a lover to his former mistress, it relates his escape from the bonds of love, earthly ambition, and intellectual knowledge – an escape which led him to the point where he lost and found himself in God.
[31] Cf. Febvre, *Le Problème de l'incroyance au XVIe siècle*, pp. 301-302: "Dieu, annonce Luther ... est l'auteur unique du salut. Dieu |seul, entièrement et absolument: car l'homme peut bien entraver l'œuvre de justification, la seconder, ou l'aider: mais y collaborer en quoi que ce soit, jamais.... Que l'homme ... reconnaisse ... qu'il est incapable de rien faire lui-même pour son salut; alors la Grâce s'abaissera vers lui spontanément. Elle éveillera la Foi – qui elle non plus, ne naît pas d'un effort de l'homme...."
[32] Quoted in Jourda, II, 1047.

possessed of supreme love, he cannot, acting instinctively and spontaneously, commit any sin. And the last concludes that the sinner cannot be reformed: since sin is possible only with God's permission, to fight it is a sign of pride and insolence on man's part. Therefore, La Ravie knows only love; she is a 'natural' being – a shepherdess – and is totally indifferent to the world around her.

Libertinism, then, presented Marguerite with an ideal which her dissatisfaction with purely rational answers found attractive, and her familiarity with the Hermetic books, the works of Pseudo-Dionysius, Nicolas da Cusa, and the Neoplatonists, prepared her to receive it with sympathy.[33] An ideal, however, is not a program, and the Queen cannot have been insensible to the dangers of such a doctrine, even had she not read Calvin's scathing attack on the sect.[34] We must remember that La Ravie is only one of four characters, and nothing in the play leads us to conclude that hers is the only true way to God, or, for that matter, that is it practicable for all. Ideally, perhaps, we should all follow her; but the *Miroir* had already announced Marguerite's awareness that the plenitude of divine love was not to be reached in this life:

> Or icy bas ne puis parfaitement
> Avoir ce bien, qui me fait ardemment
> De tout mon cœur en desirer l'yssue,
> Sans craindre mort....[35]

[33] *Théâtre profane*, pp. 261-262.
[34] "Mais la réponse aux Libertins, verte et directe, vint en 1545, avec le petit traité *Contre la secte phantastique et furieuse des Libertins qui se nomment spirituelz*. Il n'avait pas de mal à montrer comme leurs tendances risquaient d'aboutir à un nouvel amoralisme. S'il n'est que de s'en remettre à la possession de l'esprit, sans orienter le moins du monde son attention vers ce qui est des actes, en renonçant à toute forme de jugement, on abolira par là même les deux notions de responsabilité et de sanction, sans lesquelles la morale s'écroule: on s'en remet si bien à la Providence que 'nul ne devra plus faire conscience de rien,' et qu'il 'n'est point licite de rien condamner.'" Saulnier in *Théâtre profane*, p. 251.
[35] *Miroir*, p. 53.

No doubt Marguerite believed that this 'good' was to be found only in the total surrender of the self to God, and that "ni le matérialisme et l'indifférence de la Mondaine, ni les pratiques machinales de la Superstitieuse, ni la foi un peu orgueilleuse de la Sage ne donnent à l'âme la paix qu'elle désire.'[36] Nonetheless, it seems unlikely that La Ravie's "Je ne sçay rien sinon aymer" represents, as Jourda would have it, the synthesis of Marguerite's ideas on the eve of her death,[37] even though it may indeed express her emotional preferences. Lefranc for once comes closer to the truth when he writes that perhaps Marguerite did not care to come to a final conclusion in this play, and that she was not loath to grant a parcel of truth to several of the systems she put on the stage. "Ennemie de tout dogmatisme étroit, elle excelle à mettre en relief les multiples aspects des choses, se refusant, dans son large et généreux esprit de tolérance, à lancer l'anathème contre les opinions qu'elle ne partage pas."[38]

As a matter of fact, since La Sage and La Ravie between them share Marguerite's personal ideas, neither is to be ruled out of court. La Ravie picks up the doctrine of justification by faith, the idea that love, the supreme aspect of Being, defines the path to salvation,[39] the notion that to die a mystic death is to be reborn,[40] and the theme that it is useless to proselytize since no one will listen.[41] La Sage, on the other hand, insists on the dignity of the body,[42] on the need for discussion,[43] the importance of the Bible, and the merit of works and ritual.[44] If we are therefore to describe

---

[36] Jourda, I, 605.          [37] Jourda, I, 605.

[38] *Dernières poésies*, 'Introduction,' p. xxxiii.

[39] Cf. "Aymez amours, ou soyez sourds," in *Dernières poésies*, p. 324.

[40] Cf. "Amour enfin me resuscite," in *Dernières poésies*, p. 340; also the surrender of *Rien* to *Tout* in Book III of *Les Prisons*.

[41] Developed in *Trop, Prou, Peu, Moins*, in *Théâtre profane*, q.v.

[42] Cf. also *Prisons*, p. 228.

[43] Where the *Chansons spirituelles* in *Dernières poésies* are lyric effusions, the long poems (*Les Prisons, La Navire*) seek a rational basis for faith.

[44] Marguerite herself endowed monasteries, reformed convents, and faithfully attended mass – in bed, if necessary.

the Queen of Navarre's religion, we must recognize that she was far from having withdrawn into mystic quietism. It is the tension between the lover of the absolute and the intelligently devout thinker – the very tension which animated her spiritual life – that lends vitality to the play. Marguerite is La Sage, tempted by La Ravie but not entirely convinced, and her true religion, "ce n'est pas le quiétisme, c'est, si l'on peut dire, l'inquiétisme."[45]

Jourda makes the mistake it is all too easy to make when one studies Marguerite. The *Comédie de Mont-de-Marsan* is not an essay in theology but a confrontation of values in the medium of drama. Two of its characters, as we have seen, are manifestations of doctrinal positions and are useful in determining the nature of its author's religious beliefs; the other two, however, are human types and must not be overlooked simply because they are neophytes in the doctrinal controversy. One of their functions no doubt is to act as foils to their teacher and provoke her to expose her evangelistic doctrine. But they are not entirely mechanical creatures, and they stand as representatives of what is, after all, the bulk of mankind, since worldly self-centeredness and narrow-minded pietism are more common than either intellectual idealism or mystic rapture. These two ladies may be misguided in their views, yet they are open to instruction and able to change because they are human, and Marguerite loves the human. It is this human quality that makes them respond where La Sage cannot. Thus it is that when La Ravie makes her entrance, they are concerned for her welfare, whereas their theoretical-minded teacher can only register disapproval: La Mondaine points to the girl's *song*; La Superstitieuse is dismayed by its contents; but La Sage taxes the shepherdess with madness. When the worldly lady suggests that they accost her, it is La Sage who gives up first and calls the retreat. Although La Superstitieuse follows her shortly, La Mondaine persists with confidence and succeeds in engaging the shepherdess in conversation, thus making the other two turn back. In the

[45] Saulnier, in *Théâtre profane*, p. 266.

area of human relations, curiosity and worldly tolerance are more effective than abstract systems of values. That truth the Queen of Navarre, emissary extraordinary for Francis I, had no reason not to know.

There are two orders of values operating simultaneously in the play; it is their interaction which reveals the complexity of Marguerite's thought. In the idealist hierarchy provided by the libertinists and the Neoplatonists,[46] La Ravie stands at the top, closest to God, followed in descending order by La Sage, La Superstitieuse, and La Mondaine – the more one is attached to the world and the flesh, the further down one's place on the scale. But from the point of view of what we might term purely human values – the values of the humanist educators of the Renaissance – it is La Mondaine who shines most brilliantly, followed by La Superstitieuse and La Sage, while La Ravie falls altogether outside the scheme. For La mondaine is closest to the ideal of harmonious balance of the flesh and spirit; her initial indifference to spiritual values is more easily overcome than her superstitious companion's aberration,[47] and once she converts she retains the open-mindedness that worldly experience has taught her and is therefore able to communicate with the enraptured shepherdess where the other two fail. La Sage may possess the true doctrine, but it is the worldly lady who lives it most gracefully because she knows better than her two companions how to live in the world. For that matter, even La Superstitieuse leads an active life; her notions may be erroneously perverse and difficult to overcome, but once she sees the light she is ready to temper her religious zeal somewhat,

---

[46] It should be noted, however, that La Superstitieuse does not fit into the Neoplatonist scheme, which took a philosophic, non-theological view of man's relation to God and did not concern itself with the question of ritual and works. On Neoplatonism and Marguerite's indebtedness to it, see below, Chapter II, pp. 43-49, 56 ff.

[47] Her conversion comes first, ll. 249-348; La Superstitieuse resists longer, and when she does accept the new doctrine, ll. 393-559, she still has reservations, ll. 558, 667.

and she is the one who first tries to elicit a response from the shepherdess.[48]

La Sage and La Ravie reflect the speculative side of Marguerite's nature, but La Mondaine and La Superstitieuse are closer to the active, experienced Queen of Navarre. In short, all four ladies are part of Marguerite, and it is their interrelationship that expresses her vision of human existence. She rejects religious bigotry and materialistic amoralism as unworthy of man; she hesitates between the enlightened rationalism of La Sage and the passionate mysticism of La Ravie; but in the final analysis she is working for a synthesis of what is best in each. This synthesis was never intellectually realized by Marguerite; it is, however, artistically envisioned in the *Comédie de Mont-de-Marsan* and, more successfully, in the *Heptameron*, where the dialogue form imposes unity on the disparate and contradictory elements of intellectual discourse.[49]


PART III

If there is one theme which consistently runs through Marguerite's works, it is the primacy of love in the scheme of existence. It appears not only in the religious and moral works, but also in the sizable body of courtly poems and *vers de société* she produced from the time of Marot's arrival at court, where his polished, witty verse gave strong impetus to the appreciation of poetry as an ornament of elegant living. The king's sister did her share of rhyming the events of the court, but since the decorative function of poetry interested her very little, she soon turned to the subject closest

---

[48] La Mondaine is the one who first suggests accosting La Ravie, and the one who succeeds in making her talk to them, but La Superstitieuse's zeal for reforming people is still operative and she is therefore the first to speak to the girl.

[49] "Marguerite affectionna toujours la forme du dialogue, comme plus propre qu'aucune autre à exprimer toutes les nuances de sa pensée, sans la mettre dans l'obligation de formuler des conclusions explicites sur les questions qu'elle abordait." *Dernières poésies*, 'Introduction,' p. xxxiv.

30

to her heart – love. She therefore sang the intellectual love of the idealist tradition, essaying a definition of its mystery in a series of *dizains* entitled, appropriately enough, "La distinction du vray amour,"[50] developing its plaintive aspect in the *Epîtres* and *La Coche*, but always focusing on the consequences of passion for the human beings involved.[51]

Although Marguerite was interested in ideas, she was too deeply involved in the affairs of her world, too strongly committed to those she loved, too intensely fascinated by human character ever to achieve true intellectual detachment. She kept her feet firmly planted on the ground and observed the world around her. She reported on it, interpreted it, and preached to it, seeking all the while a philosophy for living, not a metaphysical interpretation of the cosmos. It is, therefore, no accident that her finest work, her one true masterpiece, should be a work of prose.[52] Shaking off the restrictions of the lyric posture which was essentially foreign to her nature, she could express her sense of the multiplicity of human experience, and the medium of conversation further freed her, too, from the requirements of doctrinal consistency which cramp her style in the plays and the didactic poems. Conversation, as we have noted, was the life-blood of her intellectual develop-

[50] In *Dernières poésies*, pp. 301-312.

[51] The terms used are those to be found in courtly poetry and in the vocabulary of petrarchism, but the interest is focused on the human drama: even the *Distinction du vray amour*, which opens with the conquest and assimilation of human love by the divine (Marguerite distinguishes between 'Amour' and 'amour'), from the fourth dizain on develops into a debate between a lover seeking his lady's favors and the lady who insists he follow her example and turn his thoughts toward heaven.

[52] The *Heptameron* first appeared in a truncated version, in 1558, under the title of *Histoires des amans fortunez*. The following year saw the publication of the complete text, dedicated to Jeanne d'Albret, bearing an exhaustively explanatory title page: *L'Heptaméron des nouvelles* de très illustre et très excellente Princesse Marguerite de Valois, Royne de Navarre, remis en son vray ordre, confus auparavant en sa première impression et dédié à très illustre et très vertueuse Jeanne de Foix, Royne de Navarre, par Claude Gruget, parisien. – Paris, J. Cavellier, 1559.

ment; a social art, it leads to insight rather than final conclusions.

The idea for a collection of tales probably came to Marguerite when she was following the progress of Le Maçon's translation of the *Decameron*.[53] She imitated the Italian model; but to Boccaccio's narrative framework she added the brief conversations in which her narrators comment on the stories they hear. Her form not only 'imitated' the work she knew, but also provided her with the opportunity to express her moralist's view of human conduct.[54] Although her interlocutors, modeled on her intimates,[55] voice differing and conflicting points of view, they share

[53] Antoine Le Maçon's translation of the *Decameron* appeared in 1545; there is evidence that Marguerite watched closely the progress of that translation (see Jourda, II, 669-685). Jourda, *Répertoire*, lists two letters having reference to Boccaccio's first novella( Nos. 351 and 772) and quotes from the latter, addressed to Le Maçon: "Je vous prie, Monsieur, m'envoyer la traduction de la première nouvelle se trouvant au roman de Boccacio le Florentin concernant messire Chapelet du Prat, considéré en son vivant comme méchant et qui, après sa mort, fut réputé saint, sous l'invocation de Saint Chapelet. J'ai besoin de cette traduction le plus tôt possible."

[54] The French humanists of the earlier sixteenth century were all moralists, and Marguerite was no exception. Cf. C.-A. Mayer, *La religion de Marot*, p. 134: "Pour comprendre les hommes de la Renaissance, il faut adopter le point de vue qui était le leur, le seul, selon eux, qui eût une valeur réelle, la morale. Ni la scolastique, ni la théologie, ni même le platonisme ressuscité ne sauraient nous révéler la pensée d'un Rabelais ni d'un Bonaventure des Périers. *Pantagruel* et *Gargantua*, comme le *Cymbalum Mundi* manifestent une incompréhension totale de toute philosophie non morale, quand ce n'est un refus de la métaphysique et du dogmatisme. Il en est de même de la poésie de Marot.... Malgré son mysticisme et son engouement pour le platonisme, Marguerite de Navarre reste profondément préoccupée par la philosophie morale."

[55] Oisille stands for Louise de Savoie, mother of Marguerite and François; Hircan, for Henri d'Albret, Marguerite's second husband; Parlamente, for Marguerite herself; Longarine, for Aimée Motier de La Fayette, dame de Longray; Dagoucin, for Nicolas Dangu, bishop of Séez and Mende; Saffredent, Jean de Montpezat, husband of Françoise de Fimarcon, who appears as Nomerfide; Ennasuitte, for Anne de Vivonne, wife of François, Baron de Bourdeille (who appears as Simontault), mother of Brantôme, lady-in-waiting to Marguerite; Geburon, for the seigneur de Burye, the king's commander in Guyenne and member of Marguerite's circle after 1540. Not all identifications are certain;

her ideal of an enlightened humanism and a liberal evangelism; their clashes thus enrich the synthesis of the ideal and the real Marguerite had always sought. It is in this, her one truly popular work, that the Queen of Navarre gives us the most complete statement of her moral and intellectual vision.

see *L'Heptaméron*, Michel François, ed. (Paris, n.d.) pp. 447-448, notes 4, 12, 13, 14, 15, 16, 20, 21, and 23. All quotations and references, unless otherwise noted, are drawn from this edition.

# CHAPTER II / THE WAYS OF LOVE

In order to appreciate the full value of the *Heptameron* one must be familiar not only with the sources of Marguerite's thought in her personal life, but also with the literature of love available for her perusal. Beginning with the poetry of the troubadours, which first made its appearance in the eleventh century, European poets built a tradition with romantic love as its central theme. At the heart of this profound interest in love – an interest which dominated the imaginative life of Western Europe for centuries, conditioning both the contents and form of its literature – lay an idealizing fantasy which attempted to deal with the conflicting demands of man's eroticism and his morality. As the literature evolved, the fantasy was spiritualized, intellectualized, and rationalized until its source in the ambivalent feelings of human beings caught between the dictates of conscience and the driving force of sexual appetite was no longer apparent; yet each modification sought to resolve the conflict through its definition of love.

To credit the troubadours with the invention of romantic passion is, as Professor Valency suggests, to imply that "what the troubadours expressed represents, not merely a new literary fashion, but a psychic posture which had not before existed in the history of our culture."[1] However, the attitudes formulated and, we might say, institutionalized by the poets of Provence "must have existed everywhere and always, a basic attribute of human nature."[2] What those poets did was to create a literary pattern reflecting the social reality and idealizing fantasies of their society.[3] Essentially,

[1] Maurice Valency, *In Praise of Love* (New York, 1958) p. 1.   [2] Ibid., pp. 5-6.
[3] For the history of Provençal poetry, see A. Jeanroy, *La Poésie lyrique des troubadours* (Toulouse, Paris, 1934) 2 vols. For an interpretive discussion of troubadour poetry and its heir, the poetry of the *stilnovisti*, see Valency, *op. cit.*

34

this pattern provided an outlet for the erotic wishes of man while incorporating the social and moral prohibitions against their unregulated fulfillment. Such a pattern naturally echoed the psychological situation encountered in life, for the tabus which stand in the way of immediate gratification have always been internalized by the psyche. Consequently, although it is quite true, as Mr. Valency shrewdly points out, that "psychologically, the lady who says yes comes first"[4] – i.e., the first step in the elaboration of the erotic fantasy stages an acquiescent woman, she inevitably becomes the lady who says no, for a socially acceptable fantasy cannot openly flaunt deeply rooted social and psychological prohibitions. But with the obstacles to the fulfillment of desire an integral part of the pattern of love, the poets were free to elaborate on the theme of infinite yearning, which became the hallmark of romantic passion. The lady became idealized; although real, she was unattainable because she was the embodiment of perfection as well as the lover's social superior, and the whole purpose of the lover's life lay in his desire to attain that perfection. His suffering was therefore a proof of his nobility of soul, and his adoration of the lady was what motivated his greatest deeds of valor. But essentially his posture was lyric, hence subjective. His love was the source of inspiration for his life, and although the world of reality which surrounded him was not absent from his poetry, it was viewed in the light of his intensely passionate feelings.

The troubadours did, however, insist on some measure of gratification. The poet's lady was not far removed from the flesh-and-blood ladies of Provençal society, and the literary activity of the troubadours became an elaborate game balancing private desire against social restriction, for the 'lady' was invariably married. The guerdon, or *don de merci*, to which the lover aspired ranged anywhere from a chaste kiss to the lady's total surrender; as Andreas Capellanus explains in his *De amore*,

---

4 Valency, p. 73.

love is a certain inborn suffering derived from the sight of and excessive meditation upon beauty of the opposite sex, which causes
each one to wish above all things the embraces of the other and by
common desire to carry out all of love's precepts in the other's
embrace.[5]

The statement is classic in its definition of passion as suffering and
its recognition of the sexual nature of desire. In a subsequent passage Andreas elaborates by distinguishing between what he terms
'pure' and 'mixed' love, the first dispensing with physical consummation, the second culminating in "the final act of Venus."[6]
'Pure' love is preferable, but 'mixed' love is praiseworthy, too,
although it manifestly presents grave dangers since it threatens to
jeopardize the lovers' standing with both God and society. The
literature of *fin amor* thus failed to solve the problem inherent in
human love, but it mitigated the moral condemnation attached to
illicit love affairs by incorporating them into an idealized pattern.
It exalted private passion as the source of all that is good and desir-
able in life and canonized the true lover, the *fin aman*, as the model
of human excellence. Once the goal of love was definitively
deflected from possession to worship, sexual consummation could
be viewed as an inconsequential slip from perfection which did not
necessarily invalidate the basic pattern, since the obstacles to full
enjoyment were ever present.

As long as the affective life of the lover was centered on desire
rather than on its gratification, the idealism of true love was not
destroyed. The doctrine of true love created an image responsive
to the psychic and social pressures of its time, an image which
catered to its courtly audience's most cherished dreams. Nonetheless, it remained firmly attached to the realities of this world,
however much it idealized them. Consequently, it left room also
for the very compromises between private desire and conventional
morality upon which men and women have always acted.

[5] Andreas Capellanus, *The Art of Courtly Love*, John Jay Parry, trans. and ed.
(New York, 1941) p. 28.
[6] Andreas, p. 122.

As long as it remained tied to some notion of earthly fulfillment, the theory of love could develop no further. Its highest goal was the perpetuation of a gravitational relationship in which the lady acted as the sun and her lover as an orbiting planet. But once the purely human situation was sublimated, romantic passion became the object of infinite elaboration and refinement. This process, begun in late Provençal poetry, was fully accomplished by the stilnovist poets of Italy, who took the idealized lady of the troubadours and abstracted her right out of existence. Removing her from the world of reality, they made her an integral part of the lover's dream:

> The troubadour lady has a certain solidity which supports the given characterization. She is remote, but she is existent. The stilnovist lady exists chiefly in the lover's heart. It is there that she is contemplated, not in the world of light and shade; therefore she takes on her various semblances with the fluidity of thought. She is now an angel with laughing eyes, now a wolf, ravenous and fierce. It is obvious that the poet is concerned chiefly with states of mind, his own mind, not with objective things. The beauty of the lady is a reflection of the poet's desire; her cruelty is a projection of his aggression. The poet describes himself first and always. Ultimately, this poetry has little to do with women.[7]

The poets of the *dolce stil*, trained in the scholasticism of the medieval universities, developed and exploited the theme of intellectual love. *Fin amor* became divested of its physical component, and all that remained was an intellectual passion for a spiritual beauty which stemmed ultimately from God; sensual desire, with its attendant fears and exaltations, was sublimated into a spiritual, mystical yearning for the absolute, embodied in the person of the lady. "To the fever of the flesh succeeded the fever of the mind."[8] Stilnovism directed love to the contemplation of the divine light reflected in the beauty of the lady, thus disposing of the social and moral difficulties encountered in a doctrine which based love on

[7] Valency, p. 210.       [8] *Ibid.*, p. 235.

adultery. To make the intellectual nature of this love unmistakably clear, the lady conveniently died and was removed to heaven, whence her benign influence could operate all the more fully as it was unhindered by the presence of the flesh. Her death caused cataclysmic upheavals in the lover's psyche, but it was needed if the lover was to understand the true nature of his passion, a passion intended to draw him to God.

Only Dante, among the stilnovists, developed the theme of heavenly ascent to its climactic conclusion, and the vision of the triune God at the heart of the mystic rose vouchsafed him at the end of *Paradiso* is the ultimate validation of the anguish and despair suffered by all stilnovist lovers. As Dante substitutes for the reality of the lady the reality of God, love, in the *Commedia*, becomes a truly cosmic force which sustains a unified vision. This vision enables Dante to see the phenomena of existence as fully real and related to a transcendent reality which places them in their proper perspective. The highly subjective passion of Beatrice's lover in the *Vita Nuova* is thus transformed into an objectively real force which leads him to an all-encompassing vision of the true nature of the universe.

If the troubadours gave literary form to an erotic fantasy, setting it in the context of a courtly society and giving desire a social goal; if Dante, under the influence of medieval Christianity, sublimated it into a transcendent vision of existence, Petrarch used it to express the drama of his inner life, the drama of a conscience no longer firmly rooted in a transcendent absolute. Like the stilnovists, he sublimated the erotic fantasy; unlike them, however, he was unable to relate its action convincingly to a genuine ascent heavenwards. His *Canzoniere* thus marks a return to an earthly setting, but this setting is no longer socially defined. Nor are the lover's goals clearly defined: Laura is the symbol of an idealism which takes its point of departure in the complex network of Petrarch's ambitions and desires; she is neither a real lady nor the incarnation of a cosmic reality. She is an angel, but an angel without a heaven, and the only goal to which she can lead her lover is the contemplation of his emotional state. The point has been frequently argued that the *Rime* contain hints of a heavenward ascent, but a careful reading of the poems collected under the heading "In morte di Madonna Laura" reveals that even after her death Laura does not effectively lead her lover to God. It is to the Blessed Virgin that he turns, at the close of the *Canzoniere*, for help in reaching heaven.[9]

In the *Rime* Petrarch was unwilling to abandon the world and its reality – Laura's very name, derived from the laurel crown of classical antiquity, is evidence of his attachment to the earthly – because he was unwilling or unable to part with the immediacy of his subjective experience. His desires were all he knew with certainty; and although he was well aware of the contradictory nature of human wishes, he could not forgo them, for they were all he had. He captured his transitory moods and set them down in sonnets, accenting the purely private nature of affective states. Passion was still conceived as spiritual in that it was not directed to the satisfaction of the senses, but because it was bereft of both social and metaphysical support, it cut the lover loose from anchorage in any sort of objective reality to set him adrift on the sea of his contradictory emotions. He was left to create his ideals on his own, to define his goals in terms of his individuality.

The *Secretum* and *Trionfi* clarify the role assigned to Laura in Petrarch's spiritual life; they also help define the nature of his relationship to the Absolute. In the *Secretum*, a set of three imaginary dialogues with St. Augustine, Petrarch asserts that it is his love for Laura which has led him to virtue and honor, but Augustine, while willing to grant him his contention, nonetheless urges upon him the far greater importance of his soul's salvation; he therefore asks him to abandon his earthly passion. Unlike Dante, whose Beatrice led him directly to heaven, Petrarch is thus faced with the dilemma of choosing between his love and his eternal welfare, i.e., between his subjective convictions and absolute truth. This choice he

9 See "Vergine bella," *Rime*, no. 336.

refuses to make: although he admits the force of his interlocutor's argument, he declares himself unable to resist his old bent for study and merely joins in with the saint's pious hope that God may yet lead his steps into the ways of truth.[10]

It is in the *Trionfi* that the dichotomy of worldly and Christian goals was finally resolved. In these poems, Laura's beauty, chastity, and virtue are no proof against death, which conquers all, and even fame, which promises man a life beyond his mortal span, is reduced to nought by the inexorable march of time. Contemplating the ephemeral nature of man's earthly experience, Petrarch realizes that only God holds out the promise of eternity.[11] In His abode Petrarch may hope to find a transfigured Laura; it is there, too, that his love will be justified as her blessed beauty is fully revealed to the host of the saved. The stilnovist pattern was thus fulfilled, in the sense that the lover finally achieved a glimpse of Heaven's truth. But whereas Dante, confident of God's presence and action in the world, had been possessed of a certainty which enabled him to stage his own ascent, Petrarch, lacking such magnificent assurance, could only express the hope that his passion would be redeemed in heaven. For however much he might proclaim the ultimate triumph of eternity, Petrarch remained at heart an earth-bound being whose ideal hovered mid-way between heaven and earth – Laura, although more diaphanous than the

---

[10] Dante, too, had a bout with 'study': the *donna pietosa* with whom he sought consolation for the death of Beatrice (*Vita Nuova*, xxxvi-xxxvii) is later identified with Philosophy (*Convito*, II, xiii). Nonetheless, Beatrice rescues him, sending Virgil to be his guide until she takes over in the Earthly Paradise atop Mount Purgatory. (Her reproof [*Purg.*, XXX, 130-132] may have reference to his infatuation with the *donna pietosa*.)

[11]     "Dapoi che sotto 'l ciel cosa non vidi
         stabile e ferma, tutto sbigottito
         mi volsi al cor e dissi: 'In che ti fidi?'
             Rispose: 'Nel Signor, che mai fallito
         non a promessa a chi si fida in lui....' "
                                    (*Triumphus Eternitatis*, 1-4)

troubadour lady, still lacked the cosmic solidity of the true *donna angelicata*. She inspired her lover to a noble idealism, but did not personally guide him to heaven. True, her death intensified his suffering by confronting him with the brutal fact of the impermanence of earthly phenomena, but he had only himself – his feelings and intelligence, rooted in his physical being – to help him in his search for an absolute. Consequently, even the *Triumphus Eternitatis* voices a hope far more than it states a certainty.[12]

Petrarch's descants on his earthly passion set the style for the idealist love lyrics of the Renaissance.[13] Boccaccio, for his part, carried Petrarch's earthliness one step further by carnalizing passion. Just as Petrarch was unable to deny the demands of his ego, Boccaccio was temperamentally incapable of excluding sensuality from his romantic dream. The *Amorosa Visione*, for instance, written under the influence of the *Commedia*, depicts a vision granted the poet under the guidance of a lady cast in a role similar to that of Beatrice. But where Dante's vision was sent him by the Virgin Mary, Boccaccio's is sent by Cupid. After witnessing the Triumphs of Wisdom, Fame, Love, and Fortune – all worldly goods, he is about to follow his guide up the steep stairway to eternal happiness when he is sidetracked by the sight of a garden, the lure of which he cannot resist. There his guide abandons him, and he encounters Madonna Maria, who, commanding him to cast his fears aside, yields herself to him in a vision. The heavenly ascent goes out the window, and the sensual component of love

[12] Cf.:  "Ma tarde non fur mai grazie divine;
in quelle spero che 'n me ancor faranno
alte operazioni e pellegrine."
(ll. 13-15)
[13] "It was Petrarch who set the fashion of ideal love for the Renaissance.... Petrarch's *Rime* were arranged as a poetic record of the uneasy ascent of the spirit through love. The influence of the *stilnovisti* upon Petrarch was profound, no doubt, but far from exclusive. Much of his verse echoed the troubadour styles directly or indirectly. Nevertheless he developed to the full the spiritual conflict which lay at the core of the new poetry, and he transmitted what was essential in terms which were generally understandable." Valency, p. 271.

41

triumphs in the sensuously suggestive setting provided by the garden. It is true that Boccaccio tries to salvage the spiritual nature of the vision by having the lady order him to return whence he came so that they might be united once more by his guide and, together, ascend the narrow path to virtue. The eleventh-hour return to virtue fails to convince, however, because the poem ends with the lovers reposing luxuriously amid flowers in that same garden before undertaking their ascent, as the poet sings:

> Amor mi diede a voi, voi sola siete
> Il ben che mi promette la speranza,
> Sol la mia vita in gioi' tener potete.
> Solo mio ben, sola mia disïanza,
> Solo conforto della vaga mente....

The close of the *Amorosa Visione* indicates the nature of the romantic dream developed by Boccaccio. The lover founds all his bliss in the *person* of his lady: she is a woman who contains, as it were, the happiness he seeks, and as she holds no reality beyond herself, she becomes the object of his desire; like Laura she arouses a passion that is private and intensely personal. Unlike Laura, however, her reality is confined to her physical existence, and her lover can possess his bliss only by possessing her. With the troubadours, possession, a symbolic sealing of the emotional and spiritual bond uniting the lovers, could be dispensed with readily; with Boccaccio it became a necessity because it was the only reality he trusted. He could not abstract spiritual or emotional values from the physically existent reality which embodied them.

It is to this insistence on the physical reality of love that we owe what is truly new in Boccaccio's treatment of romantic love: the existence of a lady unmistakably real. His Griseida, in the *Filostrato*, is a woman very much alive in her own right, with her own rationale of life, her own *raison d'être*, which do not match her lover's desires point by point. What is significant about the presence of such a character in a love romance is that it introduces anti-romantic, realistic elements which clash with the idealistic fantasy and destroy it. Boccaccio's Griseida, although she may speak the language of her romantic lover and even dream his dream, lives in a world of practical concerns. A young, beautiful widow, she must seek the security afforded by the love of a valiant knight if she is to retain her independence, and she uses her assets – her beauty and availability – to secure her ends. She is thus the ancestress not only of Chaucer's Criseyde, but of the whole gallery of court ladies who play on men's romantic dreams for profit; Ariosto's Angelica, La Borderie's Amye de Court, Marguerite's Mondaine and her counterparts in the *Heptameron* – these and countless others down to Marguerite Gautier and Odette Swann are foreshadowed by Boccaccio's Griseida.

The intrusion of this non- and at times anti-romantic point of view into the literature of love permits a confrontation of the fantasy with the reality of experience, and the reality so fascinated Boccaccio that in the *Decameron* he abandoned the romantic world for the world in which men live. It is a natural world, bounded on the one hand by the inferno of the Black Death, and on the other by the paradisiac gardens to which the privileged few make their escape. Within its confines move the men and women who, through its hundred stories, pursue their dreams, ambitions, and lusts. Boccaccio's vision encompasses a wide range of human experience, and although it provides no synthesis of material and spiritual values, Marguerite, for reasons to be considered later, chose the *Decameron*, rather than any of the other masterworks she knew, as her literary model for the *Heptameron*.

If Boccaccio often reduced love to little more than carnal appetite, Ficino, the founder of Christian Neoplatonism, sought, in his commentary on the *Symposium*, to recapture the synthesizing Dantesque vision. Reinterpreting Christian myth in philosophic terms, he established a metaphysics which unfolded the dynamic structure of Being through the primacy of the creative principle of love. He found the source of love in God and saw it as the force which cements the created universe and draws all creation back to

Him.[14] Love is a desire for Beauty, and Beauty, according to Ficino, is nothing other than the resplendence of Divine Goodness throughout the hierarchy of creation.[15] This desire expresses itself through both the intelligence of the Angelic Mind (Venus Urania) and the generative power of the World Soul (Venus Dione), the one leading to the contemplation of the Supreme Beauty, the other to the creation of this beauty in material form; these, in turn, act in the human soul as the powers of contemplation and generation, enabling the mind to recognize the divine element in beauty and ensuring the propagation of the race.[16] Ultimately Ficino came to define love as a sort of delirious seizure of the soul – 'furor' is his term – of which there are two kinds: one, physical in origin, reduces man to the level of an animal, and the other, divine in nature, intoxicates the soul of the lover and binds him most closely to God.[17]

[14] Cf. the following depiction of the universal hierarchy: "Corporis utique formam vides. Visne animi quoque spetiem intueri? Detrahe corporali forme ipsius materie pondus limitesque locorum, relinque ceter: anime iam spetiem habes. Vis et angeli? Deme obsecro non loci spatia solum, sed temporis progressum, compositionem multiplicem retine: eam protinus nacisceris. Cupis etiam dei pulchritudinem cernere? Auferas insuper multiplicem illam formarum compositionem, simplicem prorsus relinque formam: confestim dei spetiem fueris consecutus.... Fons itaque totius pulchritudinis deus est. Fons ergo totius amoris est deus." Ficino, In Convivium Platonis De Amore Commentarius, VI, xvii, in Marsile Ficin, Commentaire sur le Banquet de Platon, Raymond Marcel, trans. and ed. (Paris, 1956) p. 234.

[15] "Ceterum quid isti querunt, cum se mutuo diligunt? Pulchritudinem querunt. Amor enim fruende pulchritudinis desiderium est. Pulchritudo autem splendor quidam est, humanum ad se rapiens animum." Ficino, II, ix, p. 159.

[16] "Cum primum humani corporis speties oculis nostris offertur, mens nostra que prima in nobis Venus est, eam tamquam divini decoris imaginem veneratur et diligit perque hanc ad illum sepemmero incitatur. Vis autem generandi, secunda Venus, formam generare huic similem concupiscit. Utrobique igitur amor est. Ibi contemplande hic generande pulchritudinis desiderium. Amor uterque honestus atque probandus. Uterque enim divinam imaginem sequitur." Ficino, II, viii, pp. 154-155.

[17] Actually Ficino distinguishes four divine 'furores': "Quatuor ergo divini furoris sunt speties. Primus quidem poeticus furor, alter mysterialis, tertius vaticinium, amatorius affectus est quartus." Ficino, VII, xiv, p. 258.

44

Ontological speculation, however, is rather remote from the pursuit of happiness which absorbs the energies of most men, and the *In Convivium Platonis De Amore Commentarius*, a technical treatise in metaphysics, was beyond the comprehension of the general public. Florentine Neoplatonism was nonetheless widely influential in the sixteenth century. The dissemination of its ideas was effected primarily through the numerous literary *trattati d'amore* which popularized the new doctrine of love by shifting the discussion to the realm of manners and ideal court-liness.[18] This fusion of Christian Platonism with social grace is most evident in Castiglione's *Cortegiano*, in which the capping attribute of the perfect courtier becomes love, and the love he is to experience is none other than the metaphysical love proposed by Ficino.

Castiglione's exposition focuses on the psychic experience of the lover, and retains the key feature of any Platonic concept of love, the *scala d'amore*, which leads the lover from earthly attachments to the contemplation of God. According to Bembo, Castiglione's exponent of the process in the fourth book, love is to be defined as "un certo desiderio di fruir la bellezza,"[19] but because beauty is "un influsso della bontà divina, il quale ... si spanda sopra tutte le cose create come il lume del sole" (IV, lii), it is a spiritual entity whose appeal is to the soul. It is true that it infuses itself into created things, adorning them with grace and wonderful splendor in the manner of a sunbeam falling on a golden vase set with precious gems, but desire becomes sensual only if the lover makes an error in judgment: if, guided by his sensual perception, he comes to think that the beautiful body he admires is the chief cause of what he

---

[18] For a discussion of the *trattato* from Ficino to Bruno's *Eroici Furori* see John Charles Nelson, *Renaissance Theory of Love* (New York, 1958); for a brief discussion of the genre, see Nesca A. Robb, *Neoplatonism of the Italian Renaissance* (London, 1935) Chapter VI: "The Trattato d'Amore." Zonta has collected a number of treatises in *Trattati d'amore del cinquecento* (Bari, 1912). A fairly comprehensive listing of Italian and French *trattati* appears in Ficino, *ed. cit.*

[19] Baldassare Castiglione, *Il Libro del Cortegiano*, IV, li.

desires, he will naturally seek to possess that body. Such reasoning errs, however, because, as Bembo has it, "chi pensa, possedendo il corpo, fruir la bellezza... vien mosso non da vera cognizione per elezion di ragione ma da falsa opinion per l'appetito del senso" (IV, lii); and if the lover follows this course to the end, he will never attain the blissful contentment he seeks. For, Bembo explains, those who seek the gratification of unchaste desire arrive at one of two things: either they attain their desire and love turns to revulsion, "quasi che l'appetito si ripenta dell' error suo e riconosca l'inganno fattogli del falso giudicio del senso, per lo quale ha creduto che 'l mal sia bene" (IV, lii), or they remain the perpetual slaves of a romantic passion which can never be appeased. In either case such love is unhappy. And Bembo concludes by stating that "l'esser pallido, afflitto, in continue lacrime e sospiri, il star mesto, il tacer sempre or lamentarsi, il desiderar di morire, in somma l'esser infelicissimo, son le condicioni che si dicono convenir agli innamorati" (IV, lii).

If, on the other hand, the lover makes judicious use of the reason with which he has been endowed, he is on the way to ascend the ladder of platonic love which leads to perfect happiness because it leads to God. Let him only consider that the body is not the source, but the reflection of the beauty he desires, and he will content himself with the sight of it. Let him also love the beauty of his lady's mind, and, if his love is rational and not sensual, he may enjoy a degree of contentment by effecting a commingling of their souls through the exchange of a kiss, since the kiss is the union of both body and soul. He can then free himself from the pain usually caused by the lady's absence (since his whole joy, at this stage, consists in gazing upon her) if he will divorce her beauty from her body and keep its image in his mind to concentrate upon. His next step must be to consider the multiplicity of beauties extant in the world and form a universal concept by means of which he "ridurrà la moltitudine d'esse alla unita di quella sola che generalmente sopra la umana natura si spande" (IV, lxvii). Once he has reached this stage of generalization, he is no longer tied to one woman and no longer subject to the turmoils of romantic passion.

Neoplatonism not only denied that the suffering attached to passion is the indisputable sign of its nobility. It also freed the lover from all worldly attachments by deflecting the goal of love from a tangible object such as a lady to the inner process of philosophical contemplation. The process is rational, for the lover proceeds in his awareness of the true nature of beauty under the guidance of reason, which, at this stage in the process of abstraction from the physical world, invites him to contemplate that beauty which is seen by the eyes of the mind (IV, lxviii). When the soul perceives within itself a ray of light which is a reflection of the angelic beauty and has its source in God, it rises to its noblest part, the intellect, and sees the divine beauty. But it contemplates it in its own particular intellect only, and does not as yet fathom what Bembo calls the vast universal beauty. The final stage of this ascent is reached, no longer through the working of reason, but in a kind of mystic rapture which is an intuitive process prompted by the magnetic force of love itself:

> Quindi l'anima, accesa nel santissimo foco del vero amor divino, vola ad unirsi con la natura angelica, e non solamente in tutto abbandona il senso, ma più non ha bisogno del discorso della ragione; ché, transformata in angelo, intende tutte le cose intelligibili, e senza velo o nube alcuna vede l'amplo mare della pure bellezza divina ed in sé le riceve, e gode quella suprema felicità che dai sensi e incomprensibile. (IV, lxviii)

Neoplatonism took its point of departure from the sensually perceived world and proceeded to rationalize it out of existence in the name of a God who, deprived of the concrete substantiality with which he had been endowed by the Judeo-Christian tradition, was reduced to little more than an all-inclusive Idea. On the sensual plane it substituted the abstract concept of beauty for the beautiful lady, and on the psychological level it replaced the emotional turbulence experienced by the lover with quiescent philosophical contemplation. The *donna angelicata* of the stilnovists, who had been God's personal representative on earth, embodying the cosmic reality of the divine principle which animated the universe, and who had literally led her lover to God, became the court lady whose beauty was a mere reflection of universal beauty and who was to be readily dispensed with once her lover ascended the first steps of the ladder of love. As for the lover, whose profound psychic perturbance had been a measure of the dramatic import of his lady's presence on earth – he was asked to bid farewell to passion and assume the decorative pose of a platonizing courtier, as he contemplated the image of beauty in his own mind.

Ficino sought to restore the possibility of a Christian vision to an increasingly materialistic society, but, as Castiglione's example shows, his literary imitators reduced his idealism to the estheticism which had come to pervade polite society. The new ideal was social grace; the courtier, whose function it was to serve the Prince, not the lady, was to fashion himself into a work of art. He was to have, in the words of Count Ludovico, who draws his portrait in Castiglione's first book, "una certa grazia e... un sangue che lo faccia al primo aspetto a chiunque lo vede grato ed amabile" (I, xiv), a grace which was to be "un ornamento che componga e compagni tutte le operazioni sue, e prometta nella fronte quel tale esser degno del commerzio e grazia d'ogni gran signore" (I, xiv). Such an esthetic refinement of personality necessarily called for restraint; aggressiveness was tabu, and there was no room for strong-minded individuality – the man of *virtù* who, like Machiavelli's Prince, forged his destiny in the face of men and Fortune, and created his identity through the strength of his will. It is no wonder, then, that in a world which molds human personality into sociability the lover should be invited to shed worldly goals in order to retreat into the privacy of an inner illumination which touched no one but himself, could not be touched by outsiders, and therefore insured him a totally private source of happiness.

Bembo's exposition in the *Cortegiano* became a commonplace of Renaissance thought because it was so closely associated with the definition of the courtier as a social being, an association reflected in the majority of the *trattati d'amore* which followed Ficino's treatise. These vulgarizations of Ficino's doctrine merit little discussion, for they were written neither to discover truth nor to investigate human relations, but rather to vindicate the new social ideal. With the notable exception of Leone Ebreo's *Dialoghi d'Amore*,[20] they contributed nothing new to the discussion of love; "their fundamental ideas were taken from the works of Ficino and Pico, and the modifications that they underwent at the hands of different authors were, for the most part, of presentation and atmosphere rather than of substance."[21] The participants in these dialogues merely played an elaborate game reminiscent of troubadour play, and what mattered was the grace and elegance with which commonplace ideas were displayed. These ideas soon overflowed into the courtesy books, conversation manuals, and *novellieri* of the sixteenth century to form a stream of semi-didactic literature which could have done no more for Marguerite than to suggest the scheme of the novella-cum-discussion of the *Heptameron*.[22]

[20] First printed in Rome in 1535, these dialogues between Philone and Sophia seek to establish the difference between desire and Love, to demonstrate the universality of Love, and to show its origin. A fourth, intended to show Love's effects, was never written. The inspiration is the same as Ficino's but the goal is markedly different: "une idée maîtresse se dégage: celle de l'universalité de l'Amour.... C'est pour lui la question fondamentale, car ce qui le préoccupe, ce n'est pas tant de définir les principes de l'amour humain, mais ceux de l'amour universel sur lequel il entend fonder l'unité de l'Univers. En d'autres termes, ce qui l'intéresse c'est moins l'homme que le monde et il cherche dans l'Amour non pas le principe qui relie ce monde à Dieu, mais celui qui lui permet de se suffire à lui-même.... En fait, si son point de départ est identique à celui de Ficin, il ne tarde pas à modifier la perspective du problème et la confusion qu'il crée rendra souvent difficile la détermination des influences que l'un et l'autre exerceront." Raymond Marcel, in Ficino, *ed. cit.*, p. 120. Ebreo's interests were manifestly different not only from those of Ficino and his neophytes, but from Marguerite's as well; see below, pp. 52 ff.
[21] Robb, pp. 181-182.
[22] The interrelationship of didactic treatise, fiction, and social mores is studied in

The Queen of Navarre thus had a rich and varied literary tradition at hand for a discussion of love. Provençal poetry had defined romantic love; Dante had sublimated it into a cosmic system; Petrarch had brought it back to earth in an attempt to validate subjectivism; Boccaccio had voiced the claims of the flesh; and the Neoplatonists had rationalized love through philosophic discourse. Why, of all these, did Marguerite pick the earthiest, the *Decameron*, for her model? Boccaccio's masterpiece seems a surprising choice for a woman enamored of spiritual reality, a woman who, in the *Heptameron*, sought to reform mores just as, in earlier life, she had hoped to reform the Church, and who therefore set out to compose a course in good breeding comparable to the *Cortegiano* or Guazzo's *Civile Conversazione*. But Marguerite was a realist as well as an idealist. To achieve a successful synthesis of worldly egotism and spiritual illumination, she could not ignore, as Neoplatonism so conveniently did, the raw material of life, and to capture it she turned to the one literary genre which had become a catch-all for the rich variety of human phenomena, the novella.

The novella, an objective narrative form, belonged to the realist tradition of medieval literature, a tradition which, in its understanding and staging of human experience, took a position diametrically opposed to the postulates of the doctrine of *fin amor*. The idealist tradition was predicated on the ennobling power of romantic passion and the inherent spiritual elevation of an élite; medieval realism dwelt upon what is animal in man, an earth-bound being

Thomas F. Crane, *Italian Social Customs of the Sixteenth Century*, q.v. The love debate actually dates back to the Provençal *tenson*, a conversational verse form, and the 'demandes d'amour' in which questions were proposed (often in the form of anecdotes) and then answered. Such 'questions' also appeared in treatises, e.g. Andreas' *De amore*. (See Jeanroy, II, 247-281.) They were subsequently introduced into Italy, where they enjoyed as great a vogue as in France. The most notable literary example of the form was the 'Tredici questioni d'amore' episode in Boccaccio's *Filocolo*, a French translation of which appeared at least three times by 1550 (Crane, p. 90, n. 20). Marguerite thus had many precedents for her choice of form in the *Heptameron*.

who knows only the reality of his self-centered desires. Desire itself is nothing more than a natural appetite rooted in the physical constitution of life, and man but follows the dictates of nature when he directs his efforts toward the gratification of his appetites. As each man's nature is a law unto itself and as each man's reason is enlisted in the search for personal satisfaction, appetitive and ego drives are no longer governed by a controlling ideal of a social or cosmic order; instead, the anarchic scramble for the successful achievement of private goals becomes a source of comedy when viewed with the detached objectivity of the novella. The genre, limited to reporting the facts of human life and conduct, stages an endless series of situations involving deceived husbands, outwitting wives, clever, resourceful lovers, and parasitic monks who prey on the foibles, superstitions, and stupidity of mankind. Love is still the dominant theme, the incarnation of human desire, but it is directed to physical, not spiritual goals, for physical reality is the only truth this view of man's world recognizes.[23]

Boccaccio, in the *Decameron*, gave life and substance to a form which before him had been stylistically and structurally arid.[24] In his hands the novella became a work of art, its superficial realism transmuted into a compelling vision of the nature of existence which gave validity to the materialism of the flesh. Here lies the profound significance of the *Decameron*: in bringing the diversified

[23] On the novella, see Francesco De Sanctis, *History of Italian Literature*, Joan Redfern, trans. (New York, c1959) I, Chapters IV, IX, and XII, *passim*. See also J. A. Symonds, *Renaissance in Italy: Italian Literature* (New York, 1885) I, Chapters I and II, *passim*, and II, Chapter X: 'The Novellieri.'

[24] Here is a sample from the *Novellino*: "Della Vendetta Ke Fece Iddio d'Uno Barone de Carlo Magno." "Carlo Magno essendo ad oste sopra i Saracini, venne a morte, fecie testamento, intra ll'altre cose giudicò suo cavallo e sue arme a' poveri; e lasciolle a un suo barone ke lle vendesse e desselle a' poveri. Quelli si tenne e non ubbidio. Carlo tornò a llui e disse: 'otto generationi di pene m'ài fatte sofferire in Purgatorio per die, per lo cavallo e ll'arme ke ricievesti; ma gratia del singniore mio, io ne vo purgato in cielo, e tu lla comperrai amaramente'; ché, undenti centomilia genti, venne un trono da cielo et andonne con lui in abisso." Ernesto Grillo, ed., *Early Italian Literature* (London, 1920) II, 72.

material of the novella under the esthetic control of style, it gave its readers the delight of self-recognition in an imaginative delineation of the values they lived by.[25] In exploiting the possibilities of the *novelliere* to their fullest, Boccaccio not only created a consummate masterpiece which remains unique in the history of literature, but also defined the scope of the genre. He passed on to his successors, Marguerite included, the novella as literature.

By the authority of its example, the *Decameron* inspired countless imitations in the sixteenth century.[26] But the Italians who followed Boccaccio did not, generally, take over his coherent vision of a world founded in the flesh; instead, they bent their efforts to the elaboration of the sensational. What they did borrow, however, was the device of the narrative framework.[27] The setting for the stories coated with polite elegance what would otherwise have been an anarchic and frequently obscene world, a world peopled by men who no longer believed in a moral universe, even if they still paid lip-service to such an idea. For social breeding came to replace morality as a force for order in the *cinquecento*, and private passions, left untouched by this esthetic ideal, ran riot in literature as well as in life. The *novelliere* thus mirrored its world perfectly: Boccaccio's scheme had room for every type of human action – noble, depraved, or merely foolish, and welcomed the idealization of elegant manners and language which had superseded morality in public life. Marguerite appropriated it for her very different purposes because she saw the

[25] "Naturalism... was surging up in the fullest harmony with the feelings and the daily lives of the people, and had all the attraction of novelty. And literature was being reversed at its foundation. The romance and the tale, which had always been looked upon as vulgar and inadmissible forms, were coming to the top. And instead of the lyrical world, with its ecstasies, its visions, its legends and enthusiasms, we have the epic or narrative world, with its adventures, its festivals, its descriptions, its pleasures, and its malice." De Sanctis, I, 304-305.

[26] See Symonds, *Italian Literature*, II, p. 60; also Giambattista Passano, *I Novellieri in Prosa* (Milano, 1864).

[27] Symonds, *Italian Literature*, II, 57.

possibility of joining within it the realism of her observation of life with the idealism of her spiritual convictions.

The parallels between the *Heptameron* and its model are obvious. The *Decameron's* famous description of the plague is echoed in Marguerite's narrative of the natural disasters and human violence her sundry travelers encounter in the Pyrenees, and the abbey of Notre-Dame de Serrance, where they finally take refuge, takes the place of the country villas to which the Florentine ladies and noble youths retire. When Marguerite's aristocrats devise ways to while away the time during their enforced sojourn at the abbey, Parlamente suggests the scheme of the *Decameron*: let them relate a hundred stories over a period of ten days, and if these should be deemed sufficiently worthy, they will set them down in writing and present them to the royal family. It is here that Marguerite is explicit on her fondness for her Italian model:

> Je croy qu'il n'y a nulle de vous qui n'ait leu les cent Nouvelles de Bocace, nouvellement traduictes d'ytalien en françois, que le roy François, premier de son nom, monseigneur le Daulphin, madame la Daulphine, madame Marguerite, font tant de cas.[28]

As a matter of fact, the *Decameron* was so popular in the royal circle that, according to Parlamente, its members had planned to entertain themselves by composing a similar work:

> les deux dames dessus nommées ... se delibererent d'en faire autant, sinon en une chose differente de Bocace: c'est de n'escripre nulle nouvelle qui ne soit veritable histoire. Et prosmirent les dictes dames et monseigneur le Daulphin avecq d'en faire chascun dix et d'assembler jusques à dix personnes qu'ilz pensoient plus dignes de racompter quelque chose, sauf ceulx qui avoient estudié et estoient gens de lettres; car monseigneur le Daulphin ne voulloit que leur art y fut meslé, et aussy de paour que la beaulté de la rethoricque feit tort en quelque partye à la verité de l'histoire.[29]

Unfortunately affairs of state and the wars in Italy made the realiza-

[28] Prologue, p. 9.    [29] Prologue, p. 9.

tion of this project unfeasible; therefore let us now do the job, says Parlamente, keeping in mind the rule of veracity laid down by the royal ladies: "dira chascun quelque histoire qu'il aura veue ou bien oy dire à quelque homme digne de foy."[30]

Marguerite's insistence, at the beginning of her book, on the truthfulness of her stories, coupled with her rejection of rhetorical artistry, suggests that though she may have borrowed the narrative framework of the *Decameron*, she is putting it to an altogether different use from that intended by Boccaccio. The esthetic element, so important in the Italian work, is conspicuously absent from the *Heptameron*, an absence all the more notable because she bows to tradition to the extent of referring to the beauty of the meadow in which her characters tell their tales. Introducing it as "ce beau pré le long de la riviere du Gave, où les arbres sont si foeillez que le soleil ne sçauroit percer l'ombre ny eschauffer la frescheur,"[31] she freely acknowledges her inadequacy, adding that it was "si beau et plaisant qu'il avoit besoin d'un Bocace pour le depaindre à la verité."[32] While the comment recognizes a difference in artistic ability, it also serves to underline the profound difference in sensibility and interest which separates Marguerite from the Italian men of letters. Where they, in imitation of Boccaccio's example, delighted in the decorative function of their framework and setting, she uses it to give intellectual control and moral direction to her book. Her stories are to be taken as *exempla*; they are not, she is saying, just literary exercises for the delectation of her audience. Unlike her Italian confrères, she is more interested in the truth her tales contain – the raw material of human experience which may provide the basis for a serious discussion of ethics – than in beauty of style or sensationalism of content. Her narrators must believe in the veracity of the tales if their discussions are to deal with real issues rather than provide merely the decorous framework for an amusing pastime. Whether they be in fact true or not is irrelevant:

[30] Prologue, p. 10.    [31] *Ibid.*, p. 10.    [32] *Ibid.*, p. 10.

54

she insists that they be taken at face value because they mirror the actions and passions of real men and women.[33]

The moralist's seriousness that underlies the *Heptameron* does not make it any less entertaining a work. On the contrary, Marguerite's artistry consists in her amazing ability to capture live the tone of conversation and to suggest with a few deft strokes the moral and psychological weight of her characters. Never is she so successful as in the discussions, which carry the full didactic force of the work. The *exempla* do not have the free-flowing grace and natural explosiveness of the conversations; like her poetry, they reveal her limitations as an artist. The stories are entertaining on the whole, but they are not greatly told; the *Heptameron* lives chiefly in its conversations.

One would not wish to suggest that the Queen of Navarre, deciding one fine day to write a treatise on love, determined, upon theoretical considerations, that she needed the raw stuff of life for her study and would therefore turn to the novella for her material and form. It seems more reasonable to imagine her trying her hand at setting down some of the stories that fed the conversational life of her entourage, just as she had tried to fashion courtly poetry. In her drawing-room life and literature not only met, but merged; she lived in a semi-artificial society which had adopted the forms of social polity first projected by literature, and since the narration of events and stories became the occasion for

---

[33] Parlamente therefore introduces the tale of romantic adventure she relates on the first day with such phrases as "car mon histoire est si belle et si veritable...," "si m'a-elle esté racomptée par ung de mes plus grands et entiers amys," and "parquoy tout cela est veritable, hormys les noms, les lieux et le pays." (Novella 9, disc., p. 54.) Similarly, Oisille hesitates to relate the medieval romance of *La Chastelaine de Vergi* because "nous avons juré de ne rien mectre icy qui ayt esté escript," although she adds that it was written by an author "qui est bien croyable." (Novella 69, disc., p. 400.) As for the vexing problem of sources and the – to my mind – pointless search for analogues, one may agree with Jourda's conclusion that Marguerite owes little to her predecessors in the form of direct borrowings (Jourda, II, 749). At any rate, my concern is with the *use* to which she put her material.

theoretical debate in her circle, the form of the *Heptameron* echoes
what was in fact Marguerite's reality. Both literary practice and
the example of her social circle gave her precedent for her fusion of
the novella, the courtesy book, and the formal treatise.

Marguerite's form, then, permitted her to consider love in all
its manifestations, but not all of them are valued equally. We may
imagine the Queen musing to herself that mankind comprises
sensualists and romanticists as well as Platonists and Christians, and
all of them are to be taken into account before one can form one's
judgment of love. It is this generosity of mind, this desire, so
characteristic of Marguerite, to include rather than exclude,
which makes the *Heptameron* unique among literary discussions of
love. She will keep faith with human experience no matter how
confusing or contradictory it may appear. Furthermore, she will
stop short of final conclusions. She will put the various theories of
love to the test of action, and, having taken note of the consequences in the stories, she will allow her interlocutors to battle it out,
as they did in the *Comédie de Mont-de-Marsan*, with the weapons
which are their natural endowment – their sensibility and their
measure of reason. Her hope was, I think, that out of this clash
truth might emerge.[34]

An understanding of Marguerite's literary form and the use to
which she put it makes possible a proper assessment of the
ideological structure of the *Heptameron*. It has become a commonplace to speak of the book as if it were nothing short of a demonstration of Ficino's theories, but such a view once again ignores
Marguerite's essential eclecticism. She borrowed from Neoplatonism the spirit which sought to reconcile human love with
Christian truth just as she had borrowed from the reforming
evangelism of the Northern humanists those elements which most
suited her spiritual needs. She recognized its value for the forma-

[34] It is true that the *Heptameron* was unfinished at the time of Marguerite's
death. But the evidence of the seventy-two tales and discussions, of her plays, and
other works suggests that had she lived to complete the hundred tales, her book
would be no more conclusive than it is now.

tion of a spiritually responsive aristocracy, refined in mind and manners; she discerned, too, in the ladder of love, the one link between heaven and earth which might convincingly replace the discarded Dantesque synthesis in the eyes of her worldly contemporaries.[35] She did not, however, systematize, because to do so would have meant omitting large segments of experience, and her attachment to life in its multifarious forms – her most attractive trait, it seems to me – compelled her to opt for experience over logic. Even in the *Comédie de Mont-de-Marsan*, where the characters are not much more than animated philosophies of life, Marguerite's inconclusive dialogue, her involvement in an unresolved conflict of ideas, gives her work a richness of texture, a fullness of vision no intellectual solution open to her could have provided. In the *Heptameron*, where the reader is helped to a generous variety of amatory patterns, the confrontation conveys a sense of complexity philosophical discussion could not achieve. There is intellectual design in Marguerite's book, but it is no more than a loose framework over which the body of the work is casually hung. The Queen's worldly wisdom, enlightened by educated reflection, led her to begin with the relationship between the sexes and to clarify the nature of amatory behavior in order to define a *right* relationship. In the course of the search the book echoes the ideals of Christian and Neoplatonic doctrine. That, essentially, is the intellectual design of the work.

Hence, to see the *Heptameron* as a demonstration of Neoplatonic doctrine misses the point. To begin with, two prominent features of Neoplatonic mythology are notoriously absent from its pages:

---

[35] On Marguerite's interest in Neoplatonism, see Abel Lefranc, "Le platonisme et la littérature en France" and "Marguerite de Navarre et le platonisme de la Renaissance," in *Grands écrivains français de la Renaissance* (Paris, 1914). On her interest in Dante, see Lefranc, "Marguerite de Navarre et le platonisme de la Renaissance," pp. 241-242; Jourda, I, 371-375 (borrowings from Dante and Petrarch illustrated, pp. 374-375), 573-575; M. Mignon, "La culture Dantesque en France" and "L'italianisme de Marguerite de Navarre," in *Les affinités intellectuelles de l'Italie et de la France* (Paris, 1923).

the cult of Beauty and the spiritual ascent of the lover towards God. These are necessarily interrelated since Beauty, equated with the Supreme Good, is the magnet which draws the lover ever onward; if not for his innate desire for Beauty, he would never begin his upward pilgrimage. The novella, however, is at heart an objective reportorial form and as such does not invite the extended reflections on the nature of beauty that are the hallmark of literary Neoplatonism. Furthermore, in the *Heptameron*, discussions and stories alike say nothing about beauty as the source of the lover's desire. Ladies are chosen for their bearing, their personality, their station in life, or their mere availability. Even a cursory reading of the book will convince one that Marguerite can do without the Ficinian doctrine of beauty, and without a beginning in physical beauty there simply is no ladder to ascend.

Nor do Marguerite's lovers ascend it. The characteristic experience of the Platonic lover – the gradual ascension of steps on a ladder of love leading him to the enraptured contemplation of the beauty, goodness, and justice of God – is also absent. Instead, lovers turn to God, when they do, out of desperation, because love has proved to be frustrating and painful beyond endurance; as with Petrarch, the links between earthly and heavenly love are tenuous. As for those who content themselves with 'Platonic' relationships of one sort or another, their love is akin to the 'pure' love of the troubadours: they establish an idealized relationship and never reach the intoxicated state induced by the divine 'furores' which, in Neoplatonism, open the eyes of the soul to the vision of God. Their love, however much idealized, never transcends its earthly limitations.

What, then, is there of Neoplatonism in the *Heptameron?* If, as I have suggested, the significance of the Neoplatonic movement lay in its attempt to restore unity to a badly splintered universe, to bridge the gap which divided a secularized society from the divine essence without rejecting the purely human values in the name of which man asserted his dignity – if this was how Marguerite understood it, then, as the one transcendent system available to her, it permitted her to give full due to human goals without losing sight of the very real presence of God. In the light of a system which saw all of creation linked to its creator by love, she could discard the painful dichotomy of sinful soul and nearly unattainable God so central to the mood of the *Miroir de l'âme pécheresse* and substitute a unified vision which perceives behind the multitudinous manifestations of human desire the resplendent unity of God's love.[36] The question of how Marguerite, a sincere Christian, could pen a collection of licentious tales without awareness of the contradiction between sacred and profane love – a question which has nonplussed many commentators[37] – is thus easily answered. Christian Neoplatonism, which saw all forms of love as manifestations, on different levels, of the force that binds the universe in its several parts and joins it to God, provided an all-embracing scale, a truly universal *scala d'amore*, which, starting from instinctual appetite, reached beyond reason to the enraptured seizure of the divine

[36] Ficino's system is circular; it permits man to love himself, the creation, and the Creator in one continuous movement, so that nothing is lost, and everything is gained when he finds himself in God: "Si corpora, si animos, si angelos diligemus, non ista quidem sed deum in istis amabimus. In corporibus quidem dei umbram; in animis dei similitudinem; in angelis, eiusdem imaginem. Ita deum ad presens in omnibus diligemus ut in deo tandem omnia diligamus.... Verus autem homo et idea hominis idem. Ideo quisque nostrum in terris a deo separatus, non verus est homo, cum a sui idea sit formaque diiunctus. Ad eam nos divinus amor pietasque perducet. Cumque hic discerpti simus et mutilati, idee tunc nostre amando coniuncti, integri homines evademus, ut deum primo in rebus coluisse videamur, quo res deinde in deo colamus, resque in deo ideo venerari, ut nos ipsos in eo pre ceteris amplectamur, et amando deum, nos ipsos vedeamur amasse." Ficino, *ed. cit.*, VI, xix, 239.

[37] A common criticism of the *Heptameron*, according to Lucien Febvre, is that it concludes "sur un ton moral un conte qui offense *notre* pudeur." (*Autour de l'Heptaméron*, p. 249). He quotes the following example (p. 249, n. 89): "ce que je trouve d'*étonnant* dans l'*Heptaméron*... c'est la prétention de l'écrivain à tirer de ces récits licentieux des conclusions morales, c'est l'opposition aussi entre ce livre et les autres écrits de la princesse." (Busson, *Les sources du rationalisme*, p. 135.) Some see Marguerite's 'moralizing' as an aberration due to the habits of the times: "La reine de Navarre, sacrifiant à la mode du temps, 'moralise,' elle aussi." (Mignon, p. 157.)

'furores.'[38] It is this scheme which gave Marguerite the conceptual framework whereby she could survey the whole range of human loves without losing her Christian bearings. Essentially, Neoplatonism reinforced Marguerite's Christian view. In this sense, the work of the Neoplatonists was of capital importance to the creation of the *Heptameron*.

Marguerite did not want the world left behind, so to speak, and, philosophically, at least, Neoplatonism does not reject the world. She wanted it perfected, and in practical terms, Neoplatonism defined an ideal towards which lovers should strive, even if they fail to reach it. Marguerite's one explicitly Neoplatonist statement in the *Heptameron* is uttered by Parlamente, who, in a discussion of man's ability to love God perfectly, emits the opinion that "jamais homme n'aymera parfaictement Dieu, qu'il n'ait parfaictement aymé quelque creature en ce monde."[39] Challenged by Saffredent, she proceeds to a definition of perfect lovers:

> J'appelle parfaictz amans ... ceulx qui cerchent, en ce qu'ilz aiment, quelque parfection, soit beaulté, bonté ou bonne grace; tousjours tendans à la vertu, et qui ont le cueur si hault et si honneste, qu'ilz ne veullent, pour mourir, mectre leur fin aux choses basses que l'honneur et la conscience repreuvent; car l'ame, qui n'est creée que pour retourner à son souverain bien, ne faict, tant qu'elle est dedans ce corps, que desirer d'y parvenir. Mais, à cause que les sens, par lesquelz elle en peut avoir nouvelles, sont obscurs et charnelz par le peché du premier pere, ne luy peuvent monstrer que les choses visibles plus approchantes de la parfection, après quoy l'ame court, cuydans trouver, en une beaulté exterieure, en une grace visible et aux vertuz moralles, la souveraine beaulté, grace et vertu. Mais, quant elle les a cerchez et experimentez et elle n'y treuve poinct Celluy qu'elle ayme, elle passe oultre, ainsy que l'enfant, selon sa petitesse, ayme les poupines et autres petites choses, les plus belles que son œil peult veoir, et estime richesses d'assembler des petites pierres; mais, en croissant, ayme les popines vives et

---

[38] "L'Amour est en fait une puissance infra et supranaturelle puisqu' en fait, elle naît au niveau de l'instinct, et doit s'élever au-dessus de l'intelligence pour atteindre son but." Raymond Marcel, in Ficino, *ed. cit.*, p. 112.
[39] Novella 19, disc., p. 151.

amasse les biens necessaires pour la vie humaine. Mais, quant il congnoist, par plus grande experience, que ès choses territoires n'y a perfection ne felicité, desire chercher le facteur et la source d'icelles. Toutesfois, si Dieu ne luy ouvre l'œil de foy, seroit en danger de devenir, d'un ignorant, ung infidele philosophe; car foy seullement peult monstrer et faire recevoir le bien que l'homme charnel et animal ne peult entendre.[40]

At first glance this declaration represents the ladder of love. It is obvious, however, that what holds Marguerite's attention is the goal towards which the ladder leads, not the step-by-step process of the ascension. But what especially needs to be emphasized is that the final step can be taken only by virtue of the God-granted gift of faith; Marguerite is Christian enough to refuse man the glory of rising through his own will and understanding, and for the divine 'furores' she substitutes divine grace.[41] Furthermore, the definition does not require that the final rung be reached; it is apparently enough that some ideal value beyond the satisfaction of sensuality be sought for lovers to be on the road to perfection. In short, perfection in love is a goal to be aimed at rather than a station that is inevitably reached, and we have here not a 'progress of love' but a *scala d'amore* operating as a measuring standard for the various kinds of erotic and amatory behavior depicted in the stories of the *Heptameron*. Neoplatonism, then, not only gave Marguerite a *Weltanschauung* that organizes her material but also a scale against which to measure its particulars. In no other way is she truly Neoplatonic.

With the exception of Parlamente's definition of perfect lovers, Neoplatonism is nowhere explicitly expressed in the *Heptameron*, yet it is, I believe, an important key to the meaning of the book. As I have already pointed out, Neoplatonism was the one system

---

[40] Novella 19, disc., pp. 151-152.
[41] Marguerite may also have taken to heart Calvin's warning, sounded in the *Excuse aux Nicodémites*: "Il y a la troisième espèce [de mauvais croyants] de ceux qui convertissent à demy la Chrestienté en philosophie." (Quoted by Saulnier, ed., in Marguerite de Navarre, *Théâtre profane*, p. 145.)

available to the sixteenth century which made the conjoining of mundane and Christian ideals possible. When the Queen of Navarre reminds her readers repeatedly, if discreetly, that God presides over the activities of this world and does not shut Himself off from His creation, she is being not just a good Christian, but a good Neoplatonist as well.[42] Each day's storytelling begins with a reading from the Scriptures and the hearing of mass, and ends with attendance at Vespers. Surely, if the whole point were merely the formal obeissance to the deity on the part of worldly lords and their ladies, the traditional forms of worship alone would have sufficed. But to these Marguerite adds the Scriptural readings by Oisille, who, in the Prologue, declares that only in the Bible is to be found the true and perfect happiness of the soul whence derive the repose and health of the body.[43] Here Marguerite's evangelism joins forces with her Platonic idealism as the link between man and God is no longer found solely in the mystery of the mass, but in the mystery of love as well, the contemplation of which brings in its wake a joy which is not unlike the 'furores' described by Ficino: 'And,' continues Oisille,

> si vous me demandez quelle recepte me tient si joyeuse et si saine sur ma vieillesse, c'est que, incontinant que je suys levée, je prends la Saincte Escripture et la lys, et, en voiant et contemplant la bonté de Dieu, qui pour nous a envoié son filz en terre anoncer ceste saincte parolle et bonne nouvelle, par laquelle il permect remission de tous pechez, satisfaction de toutes debtes par le don qu'il nous faict de son amour, passion et merites, ceste consideration me donne tant de joye que je prends mon psaultier et, le plus humblement qu'il m'est possible, chante de cueur et prononce de bouche les beaulx psealmes et canticques que le sainct Esperit a composé au cueur de David et des autres aucteurs.[44]

[42] Cf. Raymond Marcel in Ficino, *ed. cit.*, p. 111: "Ainsi, Dieu, non seulement n'est pas indifférent à ce qu'il crée, mais du fait que dans cette hiérarchie, chaque membre est cause de l'être qui le suit, tout le réel se trouve du même coup soumis et entraîné par l'Amour."
[43] Prologue, p. 7: "... la lecture des sainctes lettres en laquelle se trouve la vraie et parfaicte joie de l'esprit, dont procede le repos et la santé du corps."
[44] Prologue, p. 7.

This is no more than the evangelists' program in action, and we see here the lasting influence of Erasmus and Lefèvre; yet the insistence on the contemplation of divine love and the use of poetry as the vehicle for the expression of one's joy is also in keeping with Christian Neoplatonism.[45] What is more to the point, however, is that a group of aristocrats may avail themselves of this illumination without abandoning their identity and interests as men and women of the world. True, if unconscious, disciples of Castiglione's hero, they play the roles assigned to them by their position in society, yet keep their souls attuned to a love which transcends their mortal limitations. God may drop from consciousness in the course of the day but, Marguerite seems to be saying, He is nonetheless part of their lives.

The *Heptameron* thus eschews the established forms treating of love and turns to light fiction for its form, although it still proposes to be a serious discussion of its topic. Since the novella by its very nature expresses the worldly interests and desires of its time, Marguerite's book may be considered as a work which studies love from the point of view of that corporate body known as society, if one understands that society is here thought of simply as the aggregate of individuals who are its members. Marguerite is not particularly interested in the casuistry of love,[46] nor is she particularly concerned with its passional aspect; what does hold her attention is its manifestation as action in society – the behavior of men and women acting under the compulsion of erotic drives, and the consequences of that behavior. It is thus a real psycho-sociological investigation of the nature of love that is set in motion by the Queen of Navarre's interlocutors, and its purpose is to come to grips with the paradoxical nature of this passion which can

[45] One of the four divine 'furores' is the poetic; see above, p. 44, n. 17. Actually, Florentine Neoplatonism and the evangelism of a Lefèvre d'Etaples readily complement one another since both are concerned with the reality of God's presence in everyday life.
[46] At least not in the *Heptameron*. She did play with it in her secular poetry and in some of her plays.

be at once cohesive and disruptive. As presented in the lyric and epic modes, love is a compelling power which so completely possesses the psyche of the lover as to remove him from the domain of ordinary social relationships: the fiery passion which seizes the hero ennobles him, but the very subjectivity of the passional life in which he finds his *raison d'être* in effect isolates him from society. Seen in this way, love is anarchic, socially disruptive, and, ultimately, personally destructive. From the philosophical point of view, on the other hand – and especially according to the Neoplatonists, it is a cohesive force, a universal bond acting on and through all levels of creation. It is transcendental in nature and here, too, leads the lover to individual perfection. But this perfection no longer destroys the social relationships by which man normally lives. Instead, the new perfection acquired through the action of love on the inner man is necessarily reflected in his relations with others (the whole point of Bembo's discourse in the *Cortegiano*), and the proper understanding of love will therefore be good not only for the individual, but for society as well.

Since man is by nature a 'lover,' and since love is the basis for all human relationships, which, in turn, form the fabric of society, it is the love relationship which must be perfected, and the conflict between its negative and positive aspects resolved, if the social body is to reflect the goodness, beauty, and justice of God. In other words, if man can be educated to a sort of Neoplatonic ladder of love, both he and the social world he inhabits will be more harmoniously composed than before and closer in spirit to the divine idea they contain. This belief, I think, underlies Marguerite's search for the ideal relationship between the sexes in a Christian society. The quest is undertaken in the light of a philosophic position which accepts the reality of the world and sees in this reality the seeds of a more nearly perfect state for man, a state in which he will realize more fully his own nobility and greatness. In the process the Queen focuses far more sharply on the kinds of relationships that grow out of love than on the feelings which prompt them, and then examines them on a comparative basis, setting and measuring one against another. Although she never reaches any final conclusion,[47] the discussions hint at viable ideals, and her work deserves serious consideration if only for the definition of the *problem* of love she sets forth.

Marguerite's vision embraces the reality of a post-lapsarian world refracted through the prism of human appetite and desire. Unsupported by a unifying myth (such as the one underlying the *Divine Comedy*, for instance), her vision is fragmented into so many individual instances which then become the subject of rational discussion. The examples illustrate the fallibility of man imprisoned in the flesh, and the discussions seek out a rational solution to the age-old problem of the relationship between the sexes in society. The *scala d'amore*, which ranges from sensual appetite to adoration of the divine, measures the interaction of men and women who seek happiness in one another; the idealism of the spirit tries to make peace with the reality of the flesh. In the fact that Marguerite does not arrive at a pat solution to the universal conflict lies the merit of her work: refusing to simplify the problem, she has remained true to the rich complexity of the human situation which she surveys with the sympathetic wisdom of La Sage. The fascination and beauty of man's life reside in that complexity, and it is this she has captured in the pages of the *Heptameron*.

[47] See above, p. 56, n. 34.

# CHAPTER III / WORLD OF MANY LOVES:
## THE STORIES

When Marguerite de Navarre traces the spiritual evolution of man towards communion with God in the *Prisons*, she has her speaker describe his successive liberation from the bonds of love, worldly ambition, and secular knowledge until he can lose himself in God. The *Heptameron*, on the other hand, focuses on those very bonds of earthly love that the prisoner escapes; it is neither mystical nor metaphysical in conception, but takes an enlightened look at man and his loves. It should come as no surprise, therefore, that the highest form of love on the ladder of love is scarcely represented among its stories: the love which sheds earthly attachments and leads to God is not, essentially, of this world. True, there are stories in which disappointed love causes conversion to God, and there is the story of the nun whose fidelity to her vows gives her the strength to resist the blandishments and threats of a concupiscent priest; but conversions due to unrequited love are not progressions on the ladder of love, and the nun has dedicated her life to God before her story begins. Profane, not sacred love, then, is the subject of the *Heptameron*.

There are altogether seventy-two stories in Marguerite's collection. To these, its most recent editor appends an additional five tales, three of which appeared in Gruget's edition of 1559 in lieu of the 11th, 44th, and 46th stories of the authoritative manuscript of the complete text, a fourth being another version of the 52nd story, and the fifth appearing in two other manuscripts of the period.[1] Of the seventy-two stories, eight do not in any way

[1] See *L'Heptaméron*, "Introduction," pp. xv-xvii, and "Notice Bibliographique," pp. xxi-xxvi. Marguerite left her work unfinished – she had intended 100 stories as in the *Decameron*.

involve the relationship between the sexes, and neither does one of the five appended stories.[2] The remaining cover a wide range of love situations, from the ideal of pure romantic passion to the violence of naked lust, and the narrations run the gamut from the elaborate courtly romance to the crude unadorned anecdote. There are tragic stories and happy stories, stories of betrayal and stories of revenge, stories in which women suffer and others in which men are made unhappy, stories of the deceit of husbands and stories of the trickery and foibles of wives; some told from a woman's point of view, and others from a man's; and, finally, many stories attacking the clergy. All classes of society are represented; prince, courtier, knight, burgher, servant, peasant, monk – each makes at least several appearances in the course of the seven days of story-telling. As in the other *novellieri* of the time, there is God's plenty in the *Heptameron*.

Marguerite's stories may be grouped into several categories corresponding roughly to several steps on the ladder of love: stories of lust, 'mixed' love, and 'pure' love – the broad categories into which most erotic relationships fall. To these must also be added Christian love (love of God) and a category which does not appear in the traditional *scala*: married love. Hitherto romantic love had always been defined as adulterous and had been ruled out of marriage because love is a freely bestowed gift, whereas the marital relationship is in the nature of a duty owed one another by husband and wife.[3] Such a view was in keeping with the position of some in the Church, especially those who, with Saint Augustine, took a dim view of passion, even in wedlock. Christian marriage was a sacrament symbolizing the union between Christ and the

[2] Novellas 11, 17, 28, 34, 44, 52, 55, 65, and no. V in the Appendix.
[3] Cf. the 'letter' from Marie de Champagne cited by Andreas in the seventh dialogue: "We declare and we hold as firmly established that love cannot exert its powers between two people who are married to each other. For lovers give each other everything freely, under no compulsion of necessity, but married people are in duty bound to give in to each other's desires and deny themselves to each other in nothing." Andreas, pp. 106-107.

67

Church,[4] and should not be allowed to deflect the soul from its proper path, the worship of God. "Such passion as might go beyond what was strictly necessary [for the purpose of procreation] was construed as adulterous, even in wedlock, since the husband was lovable not in himself, but only as the agent of God."[5] Yet despite the weight of tradition, Marguerite did include examples of wedded love among her stories. Not only did she illustrate the kind of affection which may subsist between husband and wife without incurring the censure of apostolic law, but she also provided examples of romantic lovers whose avowed goal was matrimony.

But the many loves studied by Marguerite are not abstract patterns to be moralized upon; instead, they appear as so many skirmishes in the ubiquitous battle of the sexes for which the over-all design of the Heptameron provides the battleground. In this war the men strive for conquest while the women fight to safeguard their virtue, or at least their honor: the eternal tug-of-war between the demands of sexuality and the curbs of morality actuates the stories. There are, of course, examples of incontinent and sexually forward women, but even in these cases the conflict between desire and propriety is apparent. At best these incontinent women deflate the ego of their lovers, and at worst they wreak havoc in the lives they touch. The ground of battle shifts in the case of the passively idolizing lover, who also finds his way into the Heptameron, but the conflict is nonetheless real, for he denies his lady's right to be a woman by turning her into an idealized abstraction. Equally

4 See Edward Westermarck, The History of Human Marriage, 5th ed. (New York: 1922) III, 328.
5 Valency, p. 24. Cf. Andreas, seventh dialogue: "Whatever solaces married people extend to each other beyond what are inspired by the desire for offspring or the payment of the marriage debt, cannot be free from sin, and the punishment is always greater when the use of a holy thing is perverted by misuse than if we practice the ordinary abuses. It is a more serious offense in a wife than in another woman, for the too ardent lover, as we are taught by the apostolic law, is considered an adulterer with his own wife." Andreas, p. 103. See also n. 46, loc. cit.

aware of the destructive narcissism of *fin amor* as of the debilitating consequences of unbridled lust, Marguerite considers both unhealthy because neither provides a proper basis for a fulfilling relationship. It is precisely the definition of such a relationship that is at issue in the battle waged by her interlocutors.

Perhaps the most conclusive evidence of the fact that the *Heptameron* is not essentially Neoplatonic is the ambiguous nature of what I have called, for lack of a better term, Christian love, where a frustrated relationship causes one or both parties to retreat from the world and turn to God instead. There are three such stories,[6] and in each case God does not so much become an object of purposeful love as a refuge and source of consolation – the lovers' retirement to the monastery is really a step preliminary to death. A passage in the sixty-fourth story is explicit on this point: the hero, having entered a Franciscan monastery, receives a missive from his lady asking him to return to her as she had only been testing him by her asperity; in reply he sends word that

> la mortiffication de sa passion extresme luy avoit cousté si cher, qu'elle luy avoit osté la volunté de vivre et la craincte de morir; parquoy requeroit celle qui en estoit l'occasion, puis qu'elle ne l'avoit pas voulu contanter en la passion de ses grans desirs, qu'elle ne le voulut tormenter à l'heure qu'il en estoit dehors, mais se contanter du mal passé, auquel il ne peut trouver remede que de choisir une vie si aspre, que la continuelle penitence luy faict oblier sa douleur; et, à force de jeusnes et disciplines, affoiblir tant son corps, que la memoire de la mort luy soit pour souveraine consolation....[7]

In the same vein, the story of Elisor's love for the Queen of Castile, who banishes him for seven years to test the constancy of his love, ends on a note of death: Elisor has renounced the world

[6] Novellas 19, 24, and 64. Novellas 9 and 26 recount the edifying Christian death of chaste lovers, and the heroine of novella 10 retires to a convent, but these endings are not central to the meaning of the stories.

[7] Novella 64, p. 385. The page references throughout are to François' edition of the *Heptameron*.

to become a hermit, and the Queen, learning of the loss of such a devoted servitor, has him sought throughout the realm, but all in vain, for "Celluy qui l'avoit retiré de ses mains le garda d'y retumber, et le tira plustost en paradis, qu'elle n'en sceut nouvelle en ce monde."[8] The same theme is sounded at the end of the story of Poline and her lover, who, finding their love defeated by the mundane considerations of their princely masters, take vows and end their lives in religious orders:

> Et depuis vesquirent Poline et son serviteur si sainctement et devotement en leurs Observances, que l'on ne doibt doubter que Celluy duquel la fin de la loy est charité, ne leur dist, à la fin de leur vie, comme à la Magdelaine, que leurs pechez leur estoient pardonnez, veu qu'ilz avoient beaucoup aymé, et qu'il ne les retirast en paix au lieu où la recompense passe tous les merites des hommes.[9]

Inasmuch as each records the frustration of passion, these three tales follow a romantic pattern: passion leads to suffering, renunciation, and death. It matters little that in one case the obstacle to fulfillment comes from the irresponsible light-heartedness of the lady, in another from the cruel pride of the Queen of Castile, and in the third from the officious interference of princely patrons who wish to see their retainers advantageously matched. Whatever their source, these obstacles insure the suffering of the lovers which, in turn, leads to the renunciation of the world, itself a prelude to the release of death. Frustrated passion may indeed be sublimated into deep and sincere love for God, but there is no evidence here of positive convergence of feeling on the deity; on the contrary, God is approached negatively, in the sense that these converts seek solace and comfort with Him but give nothing in return. Their conversion is nothing but an escape from the sufferings of earthly passion; a point freely admitted by Poline's lover when he tells her that

[8] Novella 24, p. 200.
[9] Novella 19, pp. 150-151.

pour ce que en vous voyant je ne sçaurois porter ceste dure peni-
tence, et qu'en ne vous voyant, mon cueur, qui ne peult demeurer
vide, se rempliroit de quelque desespoir dont la fin seroit malheureuse, je me suis deliberé et de long temps de me mectre en
religion: non que je ne sçaiche très bien qu'en tous etatz l'homme
se peult saulver.[10]

The motive is escape, yet love remains to plague the lovers
like a veritable devil. Thus, when the heroine of the sixty-fourth
story tries to reclaim her former lover from his monastery, he
eventually takes to his heels to flee from temptation; as for
Poline's lover, he had hoped that the monastic life would change
his heart "pour aymer autant les choses spirituelles qu'il a faict les
temporelles,"[11] yet he faints upon catching sight of her in church.
Only after she, too, retires to a convent may we consider him
safe from the terrible temptation of a love which he has apparently
not given up. Poline, it is true, hopes for a full conversion to the
life of the spirit, declaring that

Celluy qui est le vray, parfaict et digne d'estre nommé Amour,
nous a tirez à son service, par une amityé honneste et raisonnable,
laquelle il convertira, par son sainct Esperit, du tout en luy; vous
priant que vous et moy oblyons le corps qui perit et tient du viel
Adam, pour recepvoir et revestir celluy de nostre espoux Jesus-
Christ.[12]

However, the suddenness of her decision to enter the convent
suggests that her statement voices no more than a hope born of her
despair at her lover's retirement from the world. She, too,
seems really to want escape.

Elisor, in his epistle to the Queen of Castile, also bids farewell to
the flesh:

Le temps m'a faict veoir sur quel fondement
Mon cueur vouloit aymer si fermement.
Ce fondement estoit vostre beaulté,
Soubz qui estoit couverte cruaulté.

<hr>

[10] *Ibid.*, pp. 144-145.    [11] *Ibid.*, p. 145.    [12] *Ibid.*, p. 150.

Le temps m'a faict veoir beaulté estre rien,
Et cruaulté cause de tout mon bien,
Par quoy je fuz de la beaulté chassé,
Dont le regard j'avois tant pourchassé.[13]

He has discovered the rewards of a higher love which makes earthly attachments inconsequential,[14] but the end of his letter makes it clear that this discovery was prompted by his desire to escape the torments of love:

Je prens congé de cruaulté, de peyne,
Et du torment, du desdaing, de la haine,
Du feu bruslant dont vous estes remplye,
Comme en beaulté très parfaicte accomplie.[15]

And, as the ending of the story strongly hints, he, too, finds his final release in death.[16] But it is the Queen's cruelty, not his romantic love for her, which turns him to holiness.

Although the discussion following the tale of Poline leads to Parlamente's definition of perfect lovers,[17] that story cannot, either, be construed as an illustration of Neoplatonic love. The lovers turn to God because their normal, healthy wish to join in marriage has been frustrated by outside impediments and interference, not because they seek to sublimate that wish. Furthermore, their religious vows invite them to reject their attachment as a sinful error, an action not at all in the spirit of Parlamente's platonizing declaration of faith; as one commentator has pointed out, the opposition between the spirit and the flesh cannot exist in Platonic doctrine since, according to Neoplatonism, love is a desire for beauty. "Nous aimons un beau corps, puis la beauté de l'âme, puis la beauté angélique, puis la Beauté qui est Dieu. Ainsi l'on gravit cette échelle philosophique sans hésitation aucune, sans

---

[13] Novella 24, p. 199. This declaration is so far from Neoplatonic that it dismisses beauty in a very cavalier fashion.

[14] "J'ay, par le temps, congneu l'amour d'en heult / Lequel estant congneu, l'autre deffault." *Ibid.*, p. 199.

[15] *Ibid.*, p. 200.     [16] See above, p. 70.     [17] See above, pp. 60-61.

l'intervention directe de Dieu."[18] Poline, on the other hand, expects a very real intervention. She hopes the Holy Ghost will convert their love to Himself and that they will be able to reject the bonds of the flesh.

Poline's end is not suggested as one suitable for the bulk of mankind. Nor are the stories that deal with *fin amor* examples of Marguerite's ideal. Elisor, who loves the Queen of Castile, is without doubt the courtly lover of the troubadours: he loves above his station, seeks only the pleasure of seeing his lady, wishes to keep his love secret, and, when he does reveal it, asks only that the Queen accept his devotion since the intensity and perfection of his passion are sufficient satisfaction for him. His is the *fin aman*'s normal wish to be 'retained,' i.e., to become the lady's vassal in the service of love. Such a desire is often encountered in troubadour poetry, where the feudal relationship obtaining between vassal and suzerain was transferred to the love situation. This extension of vassalage was no more than a metaphor, of course, but according to its terms the lover assumed the obligation of serving and defending his lady while she, by accepting him as her knight, granted him the moral support such acceptance would bring him.[19] Elisor's aspiration is therefore in keeping with a well-established tradition when, showing the Queen her reflection in his mirror-like armor, he declares that

> il n'y a ne aura jamais aultre ymaige en mon cueur, que celle que vous avez veue au dehors de mon estomach; et ceste-là seulle veulx-je aymer, reverer et adorer, non comme femme, mais comme mon Dieu en terre, entre les mains de laquelle je mectz ma mort et ma vie; vous suppliant que ma parfaicte et grande affection, qui a esté ma vie tant que je l'ay portée couverte, ne soit ma mort en la descouvrant. Et si ne suis digne de vous regarder ny estre accepté pour serviteur, au moins souffrez que je vive, comme j'ay accoustumé, du contentement que j'ay, dont mon cueur a osé choisir pour le fondement de son amour ung si parfaict et digne lieu,

---

[18] Telle, pp. 276-277.
[19] See Valency, pp. 146-147.

duquel je ne puis avoir autre satisfaction que de sçavoir que mon amour est si grande et parfaicte, que je me doibve contanter d'aymer seullement, combien que jamais je ne puisse estre aymé. Et, s'il ne vous plaist, pour la congnoissance de ceste grande amour, m'avoir plus agreable que vous n'avez accoustumé, au moins ne m'ostez la vie, qui consiste au bien que j'ay de vous veoir comme j'ay accoustumé. Car je n'ay de vous nul bien que autant qu'il en fault pour mon extresme necessité....[20]

As fine an example of the rhetoric of *fin amor* as one is likely to encounter, the speech is designed to display the nobility of Elisor's feelings and prepare us for his subsequent despair and his ultimate conversion to the love of God. The discussion which follows this tale focuses on the folly of the Queen's action in exiling her suitor for seven years, whereby she loses a truly worthy servant, but the point of the story, as the narrator, Dagoucin, tells his companions, is that a love like Elisor's can gain nothing by being revealed and should therefore be kept concealed. It can lead only to a unilateral relationship. The pattern of the story indicates that the disclosure of passion leads to the lover's banishment, while concealment necessarily precludes any meaningful affective commerce between the lover and his lady; his ambition to be 'retained,' it would seem, is not realizable. We might hesitate to ascribe such an opinion to Marguerite, were it not for several other stories which also suggest that *fin amor* does not really work. In Elisor's case the sublimation finally achieved entails the forsaking of courtly love for the love of God. Where such sublimation does not take place, *fin amor* may be an attractive ideal, but its consequences are either disastrous or ludicrous.

The ninth story, for instance, also related by Dagoucin, tells of a petty nobleman's love for the daughter of a house greater than his. He knows he cannot marry her, and therefore devotes himself to loving her perfectly: "Parquoy son amour n'estoit fondée sur nulle fin, synon de l'aymer de tout son pouvoir le plus parfaictement qu'il luy estoit possible...."[21] The girl,

[20] Novella 24, p. 196.          [21] Novella 9, p. 49.

flattered by this virtuous love, entertains him pleasantly, until tongues begin to wag, and he is forced to forgo the pleasure of her company. When rumors of her impending marriage reach him, he finally decides to ask for her hand but is turned down because he is not as wealthy as his rival. He pines away, "sachant que s'amye perdoit autant de contentement que luy,"[22] to the point of being bedridden, and, "se laissant... aller au desespoir et à la tristesse, perdit le boire et le manger, le dormir et le repos,"[23] until he is on the verge of death. His dying request is that he may receive a kiss from the girl, whose mother orders her to comply, "voiant qu'il n'y avoit plus en luy sentiment ne force d'homme vif."[24] As he dies, he tells the girl that his love has always been so honest and pure that he never wished her to bestow on him any gift beyond the kiss he has just received, a kiss "par faulte duquel, et avecq lequel je rendray joyeusement mon esperit à Dieu, qui est parfaicte amour et charité, ... le suppliant, ayant mon desir entre mes bras, recevoir entre les siens mon esperit."[25] He embraces his love once again, this time so strongly that his heart, unable to sustain the effort, "fut habandonné de toutes ses vertuz et esperitz, car la joye les feit tellement dilater que le siege de l'ame luy faillit, et s'envolla à son Createur."[26] At this point the young lady, suddenly smitten by love, remains unconsolable. As the story has it, "le triomphe des obseques furent les larmes, les pleurs et les crys de ceste pauvre damoiselle."[27]

One can readily recognize the troubadour pattern in the tale: the secrecy of the lover caps the perfection of his worship of the lady; the *lozengiers* (gossip-mongers) interfere with the relationship,[28] and the lover suffers and pines away; the lovers meet again when he is on his death-bed, and here the lady bestows the *don de merci* (the kiss) which brings him such joy that he dies; his death opens the lady's heart to love, and she in turn is so grief-stricken that his death becomes the triumph of love (the entire death scene

[22] *Ibid.*, p. 50.       [24] *Ibid.*, p. 52.       [26] *Ibid.*, p. 52.
[23] *Ibid.*, p. 50.       [25] *Ibid.*, p. 52.       [27] *Ibid.*, pp. 52-53.
[28] On the *lozengier* in troubadour poetry, see Jeanroy, II, 111-113.

is nothing other than a variant of the *Liebestod* motif). In fact, the story calls to mind the legendary *vida* of the troubadour Jaufré Rudel. According to this fictitious biography, Rudel conceived a burning passion for a far-away princess, the countess of Tripoli, and, restless in his longing for her, joined the Crusades and crossed the seas in order to see her. He was almost dead when he reached her shores, but the countess, having learned of his condition, came to meet and embrace him. Her presence revived him for a moment, and then he expired joyfully in her arms, leaving her to grieve unconsolably over the loss of so perfect a lover.[29]

It was perhaps Marguerite's commitment to realism which caused her to introduce into her story prosaic elements which are essentially foreign to its romantic pattern. At any rate, these elements serve to put the romance in a more nearly realistic mold than that provided by the pure idealism of *fin amor*. Because the heroine is a young marriageable girl, potentially available to her lover, the story allows for the confrontation of romantic fantasy and social reality and helps delineate the purely idealistic, and, in worldly terms, impractical nature of romantic passion. It is interesting to note that the hero's love at the very start was pure and hoped for nothing beyond the pleasure of social intercourse with the girl and the privilege of adoring her; yet even he felt the intrusion of reality sufficiently strongly to try to marry her himself, once he learned that another sought her hand. Fortunately for romance, the denial of his suit comes as a timely reminder that the world of ideal love has little commerce with practical considerations; his psyche is happily forced back to its true element of pure passion unpolluted by the flesh, and the masochistic tendency of his love becomes so intensified that he chooses rather to die for his passion than to come to terms with the ways of the world. To marry the girl would not be in keeping with the kind of love he has nurtured from the very beginning; the denial of a normal relationship, on the other hand, insures the full

[29] *Les Chansons de Jaufré Rudel*, Alfred Jeanroy, ed. (Paris, 1915) p. 21.

flowering of the subjectivism which leads the hero to the exultant triumph of a joyful death. In short, this story is a telling illustration of the narcissistic nature of *fin amor*.

Other stories illustrative of the destructive force of idealized passion include the thirteenth, the story of a gallant sea captain who has fallen in love with the virtuous young wife of an elderly and devout gentleman. So smitten by her beauty and her virtue that he is rendered speechless in her presence, he declares his love only after he has left for distant wars against the Turks, in a lengthy poem sent her together with an unusually large diamond ring. In the poem he proclaims the purity of his affection and insists that all he seeks is the lady's acceptance of his profession of love. We understand that he set off for war because the lady's great virtue made him realize the hopelessness of his situation. It is only fitting, therefore, that he never learns the outcome of his suit and dies gloriously, the victim of treachery and cowardice on the battlefield to which he came because of his secretly harbored love.

One ought to distinguish between the secretiveness born of necessity and that which wishes to perpetuate the state of suspended animation induced by unrequited desire. The sea captain differs from the hero of the ninth tale in the important respect that he is a man of action whereas the latter is essentially passive. The captain makes a virtue of necessity in refraining from the active pursuit of his love; the gentleman-lover of the ninth story idealizes by choice, and the difference between the two is brought into sharp relief by the manner of their deaths, for the one willingly pines away in bed and the other, fighting to the last in an increasingly hopeless situation, dies with his boots on. The captain, an ambitious man who has made a loveless match in order to advance in the world, when confronted with the shattering domination of true love, seeks refuge from suffering in action; the hero of the other tale, with the ideal of passive adoration in his blood, commits one positive action, which hastens the death that is the only vindication possible of the noble ideal by which he has chosen to live. Yet despite so significant a difference, both heroes

77

die because of romantic attachments, and both stand as reminders of the potential destructiveness of unrequitable love.

Where such love is not destructive, it may be ludicrous, especially when it becomes a fetish, as in the case of the English 'millort' who prides himself on the lady's bejewelled glove he wears on his surtout.[30] Ostensibly told by Parlamente to give an example of an 'honest' lover, the story relates a conversation between the lord and a French ambassador. Only too glad to explain the glove because he feels it is to his praise, he informs the ambassador that he has harbored a lifelong passion for a lady that will outlast her sojourn on earth, and that, fearing to lose the pleasure of her company, he concealed his love from her for seven years. But the inevitable moment of declaration came. One day, in a meadow, the lady's sight caused his heart such palpitations that out of pity she consented to place her hand over his heart. Her kindness released a declaration of love in proper courtly terms: "Helas, ma dame, recevez le cueur qui veult rompre mon esthomac pour saillir en la main de celle dont j'espere grace, vie, et misericorde; lequel me contrainct maintenant de vous declairer l'amour que tant longtemps ay cellée, car luy ne moy ne sommes maistres de ce puissant dieu."[31]

Naturally, she withdrew her hand, but her glove remained in his, and as he had no further private conversation with her from that day on, he transferred his love to that glove, adorning it with the richest jewels he could come by and wearing it over his heart, for, as he says, "je n'ay de bien en ce monde que j'estime tant, que le sentir sur mon esthomac."[32] The terms employed by this singular lover are those of true love – there is even a trace of stilnovism in the assertion that he will continue loving his lady even after her death, yet he emerges from his story a slightly ridiculous figure. The commonsensical French ambassador, who would have preferred by far the hand to the glove, exposes the conceit of the Englishman. He shows him to be a self-indulgent poseur who has made

[30] Novella 57.    [31] Novella 57, p. 354.    [32] Ibid., pp. 354-355.

78

the idealism of true love the occasion for sentimentality and Petrarchistic exhibitionism, a poseur, moreover, whose pride misses the irony of the ambassador's comment that, truest of all the lovers he had ever encountered, he would probably have died of joy had he been granted more than the glove. A faithful adherent of true love is merely ludicrous in the light of common sense. His great passion has led him to expose his vanity instead of relinquishing his life, a situation that deflates any pretension to heroic stature. The narcissism of a passion which has no object other than itself, which denies anything resembling a genuine relationship between two persons is here not tragic but absurd.

True love, however, as that master of the obvious, Andreas Capellanus, has pointed out, does not often remain 'pure.' Nature will out and the love becomes 'mixed' with sex. The *Heptameron* takes note of the facts of life in a sizable number of stories centered on love relationships where physical consummation is attained or at least desired. In these, since morality and decorum require human beings to restrain the willful force of erotic passion, considerations of worldly position, marital status, and moral reputation make themselves felt as lover and lady engage in the age-old dance of courtship, dissimulation, and secret consummation. Because chastity is no longer the order of the day, as it was in the examples of 'pure' love, the measuring standard of the *scala d'amore* operates in this category far more extensively than in the stories already discussed. 'Mixed' love may be merely a slip from the ideal of chastity espoused on the higher level of the scale and, therefore, essentially in accord with *fin amor*, but the 'mixture' can also be so thickened as to look like lust. The extremes of density may have tragic consequences: behavior prompted by strong emotional commitments or by appetites that have gone out of control can bring about results as disastrous as those of 'pure' love. Action in the middle range of the scale, on the other hand, is merely a kind of self-indulgence, morally or psychologically undesirable, perhaps, but which leads to no catastrophic outcome.

It comes as no surprise, therefore, that the one story in which the feelings of the characters come closest to the condition of 'pure' love is also the story of a tragic love, imbued with the idealization of passion characteristic of *fin amor*. It is developed around the opposition between the requirements of private passion and those of the social world to which the lovers belong: the loyalty the lover owes his lady conflicts with the fealty due his lord. On the one side lies the world of love and night; on the other, the daytime world of social duty and responsibility. It is the attempt to have both these worlds that touches off the inevitable tragic ending, for romantic love belongs to night and darkness, and to expose it to the light of day leads to disaster. *La Chastelaine de Vergi*, from which Marguerite derived her tale, is a medieval romance which tells

> si comme il avint en Borgoingne
> d'un chevalier preu et hardi
> et de la dame de Vergi
> que li chevaliers tant ama
> que la dame li otria
> par itel couvenant s'amor
> qu'il seüst qu'a l'eure et au jor
> que par lui seroit descouverte
> lor amor, que il avroit perte
> et de l'amor et de l'otroi
> qu'ele li avoit fet de soi.[33]

The poem moves swiftly forward as it focuses on the lovers and their tragedy. Their secret love is conducted successfully until the Duchess of Burgundy, loving the knight and rejected by him, plots to destroy him by playing Potiphar's wife. In order to allay his lord's suspicions, the knight is forced to betray his secret love by inviting the Duke to observe his secret tryst. The Duke, satisfied by what he has seen, reveals the secret to the Duchess in order to put a halt to her constant nagging about the knight. She, mortified at the news, drops a hint of her knowledge to her

[33] *La Chastelaine de Vergi*, in *Poètes et Romanciers du Moyen Age*, Albert Pauphilet, ed. (Paris, 1953) p. 349.

rival, who, thinking herself betrayed by her lover, kills herself. The knight, too, commits suicide, and the Duke, infuriated by his wife's insidious actions, beheads her in the midst of her court.

Marguerite's center of interest, however, is the Duchess. Her version opens with the Duchess's intrigue, developed at such great length that it almost overshadows the story of the two lovers. The shift in emphasis is announced by Oisille's introduction to the story, when, in the discussion which follows the preceding tale, she is reminded "d'une dame belle et bien maryée, qui, par faulte de vivre de ceste honneste amityé, devint plus charnelle que les pourceaulx et plus cruelle que les lyons."[34] Marguerite, wishing to scrutinize the intrusion of the materialist world into the world of romance, transforms the thirteenth-century poem into a novella of court life. Through the elaboration of character, through the introduction of details revealing the nature of power relationships, she recreates the social and political reality she knows. The characters have all been to school with Castiglione and the humanist rhetoricians, as evidenced by the knight's reply to the Duchess's expression of amazement at his not having settled his affections on one of her court ladies: "Madame, si j'estois digne que votre haultesse se peust abbaisser à penser à moy, ce vous seroit plus d'occasion d'esbahissement de veoir ung homme, si indigne d'estre aymé que moy, presenter son service, pour en avoir refuz ou mocquerie."[35] The ornate compliment which says nothing stands in sharp contrast to the earlier work's succinct "Ma dame, fet il, je n'ai mie / encore a ce mise m'entente".[36] Similarly, the ornate rhetoric the *châtelaine* uses when she believes herself betrayed contrasts unpleasantly with the direct simplicity of expression found in the source. Here are two samples from the poem:

> Douz Dieus! et je l'amoie tant
> comme riens peüst autre amer,

[34] Novella 69, disc., p. 400.
[35] Novella 70, p. 401.
[36] *La Chastelaine de Vergi*, p. 350.

qu'aillors ne pooie pensser
nis une eure ne jor ne nuit !
Quar c'ert me joie et mon deduit,
c'ert mes delis, c'ert mes depors,
c'ert mes solaz, c'ert mes confors.

Ha ! fine amor ! est ce donc droiz
que il a ainsi descouvert
nostre conseil ? dont il me pert
qu'a m'amor otroier li dis
et bien en couvenant li mis
que a cele eure me perdroit
que nostre amor descouvreroit.
Et quant j'ai avant perdu lui,
ne puis, aprés itel anui,
vivre sans lui por cui me dueil . . . .[37]

Marguerite, handling the same situation, turns to rhetoric as she
has the lady exclaim,

O malheureuse, quelle parolle est-ce que j'ay oye ? Quel arrest de
ma mort ay-je entendu ? Quelle sentence de ma fin ai-je receue ?
O le plus aymé qui oncques fut, est-ce la recompense de ma chaste,
honneste et vertueuse amour ! O mon cueur, avez-vous faict une si
perilleuse election et choisy pour le plus loial le plus infidelle, pour
le plus veritable le plus fainct, et pour le plus secret, le plus
medisant ?... La guerre ne la mort ne m'ont osté mon amy ; mon
peché ne ma coulpe ne m'ont pas osté mon honneur ; ma faulte et
mon demerite ne m'ont poinct faict perdre mon contentement ;
mais c'est l'Infortune cruelle, qui rendant ingrat le plus obligé
de tous les hommes, me faict recepvoir le contraire de ce que j'ay
deservy. Ha ! madame la duchesse . . . ,[38]

and so the girl goes on for almost two closely set pages, to end on a
Christian note which is strangely out of place in this medieval
romance, but very much in keeping with Marguerite's bias:

Helas ! ma pauvre ame, qui, par trop avoir adoré la creature, avez
oblié le Createur, il fault retourner entre les mains de Celluy
duquel l'amour vaine vous avoit ravie. . . . O mon Dieu, mon crea-

---

37 *Ibid.*, pp. 367-368, p. 369.
38 Novella 70, p. 413.

teur, qui estes le vray et parfaict amour, par la grace duquel l'amour
que j'ay portée à mon amy n'a esté tachée de nul vice, sinon de trop
aymer, je suplye vostre misericorde de recepvoir l'ame et l'esperit
de celle qui se repent avoir failly à vostre premier et très juste
commandement; et, par le merite de Celluy duquel l'amour est in-
comprehensible, excusez la faulte que trop d'amour m'a faict faire;
car en vous seul j'ay ma parfaicte confiance.[39]

The Christian scale of values has been superimposed on the medieval code of courtliness; the original *châtelaine* had taken a very
different position when she exclaimed that the promise of God's
heaven and His paradise would not make her give up her love.[40]

The poem makes the 'mixed' nature of the love affair fairly
evident; the novella is far more confused and confusing on that
issue. The poem devotes almost a hundred lines to the meeting
of the lovers, the night they spend together, and their parting at
dawn; the novella condenses the nocturnal trysts to a laconic "il
s'en alloit parler à elle toute la nuyct,"[41] and has the knight
announce to his lady that night he can't stay long because the Duke
wishes to go hunting at four in the morning – this out of consideration for the Duke, who would otherwise be forced to keep a
night-long vigil just as his counterpart in the poem had done!
This last touch of realism was apparently necessary, for Marguerite
had no way of accounting logically for the Duke's staying hidden all
night long when one hour's observation should have been convincing enough.

Such a need for verisimilitude does not arise in the romance
because the figure of the wakeful friend guarding the lovers'
secret tryst is part of the elaborate myth constructed around the

---

[39] *Ibid.*, p. 414.
[40]     "... se tout le mont et neïs
        tout son ciel et son paradis
        me donast Dieus, pas nel preïsse
        par couvenant que vous perdisse;
        quar vous estiiez ma richece
        et ma santez et ma leece...." (p. 368)
[41] Novella 70, p. 409.

love fantasy, but in a tale which purports to be a true account of a real situation, a tale which puts the fantasy to the test of reality so to speak, mythic elements must of necessity be reduced to the level of literalism. Not only does the all-night tryst shrink to a midnight chat,[42] but the reduction to the commonplace is even more evident in Marguerite's handling of the relationship between the two lovers. She could not deny the genuineness and depth of the feeling which bound the lovers to one another, and had to recognize the nobility and worth of the attachment proudly proclaimed in the poem. But since nothing is more commonplace than an ordinary love affair, she must have felt the need to under-line the unique quality of this love by suggesting, in the heroine's valedictory, that it was all the more intense because it remained unsullied by sex. It is as if the hard-bitten pragmatic world of power relationships and court intrigue which has become the setting for the tale had killed the romance, and the only way of giving the love affair importance was to turn it into a Platonic relationship. But such a relationship, when set in a realistic context and stripped of the mythic elements of the erotic fantasy, no longer requires the dark cover of night for its continuance, and it becomes difficult for us to believe in the inevitability of the lady's death because her secret has been revealed to the light of day – the night-day antithesis no longer holds. For that matter, there is really no need for the lovers to meet in the secrecy of night, and one wonders what they did do all night long, night after night.

*Fin amor* has become so enmeshed in a net of worldly consider-ations with which it previously had little if any commerce that the lovers are left to continue in the traditional attitudes of romance without support and justification from the world in which they move. Their story demands a pattern of feeling and action which their world does not believe in; they fall back on the flowery language of rhetoric to cover up the lack of conviction in the roles they are required to play. It is not their fault if the point of focus

[42] The knight actually leaves at one a.m.!

has shifted from their romance to the intrigues of the Duchess; they are not responsible if an edifyingly Christian ending has been tacked onto their story. They cannot help but be ambiguous figures in a story which reduces poetic concept to literal statement and treats romance as if it were a chronicle. Unmistakably, Oisille's tale tolls the death knell of medieval romance. Though Parlamente voices Marguerite's wish to salvage its beauty, the Queen's attempt to tailor it for the worldly *Heptameron* succeeds only in revealing how distant the thirteenth century was from her day.

Although Marguerite's tale of the unfortunate lady of Vergi fails because it lacks a unified point of view, it still makes the point that excessive passion is destructive. In another story two lovers meet their death because of the physical enactment of their passion.[43] A young nobleman of Cremona has been wooing the daughter of some close-by neighbors but she, although she loves him, keeps turning him down. The rejection so chagrins him that he falls ill and is ordered bled by the doctors; the lady, knowing full well the cause of his illness, sends word that she is ready to grant her favors in order to cure him. When they meet that evening, he, "plus yvre d'amour et de plaisir qu'il ne luy estoit besoing, cuydant sercher par un cousté le remede de sa vie, se donnoit par ung aultre l'advancement de sa mort,"[44] for while he is making love, his bandage comes loose and he ultimately bleeds to death:

> Lors, amour, qui les avoit trop unys ensemble, feit en sorte que, en departant d'avecq s'amye, son ame departyt de son corps; et, pour la grande effusion de sang, tumba tout mort aux piedz de sa dame, qui demoura si hors d'elle-mesmes par son estonnement, en considerant la perte qu'elle avoit faicte d'un si parfaict amy, de la mort duquel elle estoit la seulle cause.[45]

Unlike the story of the *châtelaine* of Vergi, this tale is reduced to its bare anecdotal bones, and, avoiding the pitfall of ludicrousness, drives home the point that excess in love may lead to disastrous

[43] Novella 50.    [44] Novella 50, p. 324.    [45] *Ibid.*, p. 325.

results. One may be forgiven for viewing the lady's grief at the loss of 'so perfect a lover' with a certain amount of cynicism, considering how very recent, yet apparently thorough, her knowledge of his qualities as a lover must have been, and her subsequent suicide over her lover's body smacks too much of the exaggerated melodrama indigenous to the novella to be absorbed with deepfelt sympathy, but the fact remains that the story illustrates a try, however truncated, at a relationship between two people in love. The lady, we are told, did return her suitor's affection and was waiting only for some evidence of his sincerity in order to give herself to him. Once his illness proved his faith she threw caution to the wind and the passions she unleashed destroyed them both.

There are other examples of 'mixed' love which have happier endings because the persons involved are better able to control themselves. There is the story of a beautiful Milanese widow, relentlessly pursued for three years by an enterprising Frenchman who is "accomply de toutes les beaultez et graces que gentil homme pourroit avoir."[46] She flees from him repeatedly, but his persistence finally wins and she arranges to have him come to her room one night. There she tests his courage by having two maids clang swords in a closet, whereupon she pretends it is her brothers-in-law who are on the way and begs him to hide under her bed. He scorns such cowardice and prepares to fight; she discloses the truth to him, and he, cursing the chambermaids, slams the door in their faces and takes possession of the lady. It is only towards dawn that he asks for an explanation of the little comedy with the chambermaids. After explaining her wish to test him, she declares that

> pource que j'ay trouvé en vous plus de beaulté, de grace, de vertu
> et de hardiesse que l'on ne m'en avoit dict, et que la paour n'a eu
> puissance en riens de toucher à vostre cueur, ny à reffroidir tant
> soy peu l'amour que vous me portez, je suis deliberée de m'arrester
> à vous pour la fin de mes jours; me tenant seure que je ne sçaurois en

[46] Novella 16, p. 129.

> meilleure main mectre ma vie, et mon honneur, que en celluy que
> je ne pense avoir veu son pareil en toutes vertuz.[47]

Here is a woman who, smitten by an image of perfection, flees from the temptation until she is reassured on the one point that is of critical interest to her – her suitor's dependability. Hers is the realistic problem of reconciling honor with love; in that early morning confession she tells her lover that "l'honneur... ne vouloit permectre que amour me feist faire chose dont ma reputation peust empirer."[48] Now that she is sure of his trustworthiness as man and as lover – 'hardiesse' is the key word here – she can give herself freely to his love for the rest of her days; the bond between them will consist of the very freedom of the compact they have made with one another. It would seem, then, that this pair of lovers can be happy. The story, however, ends on a skeptical note as it reminds us of the mutability of human affections: "Et, comme si la volunté de l'homme estoit immuable, se jurerent et promirent ce qui n'estoit en leur puissance: c'est une amityé perpetuelle, qui ne peult naistre ne demorer au cueur de l'homme."[49] It may be that, as the Neoplatonists would have said, the very nature of the attachment makes life-long constancy impossible, although the story does not make the point explicitly. The interlocutors, in the ensuing discussion, simply take the inconstancy of man for granted and advise ladies to guide their conduct accordingly.

The eighteenth story presents another model lover whose perfection consists of his fidelity and obedience. Here, too, love has conquered; it has so flooded the lovers with its clear light "que leur penser, vouloir et parler n'estoient que flambe de cest Amour."[50] But once again, the obstacle to quick fulfillment is the lady's honor, for

> la honte qui accompaigne les dames le plus qu'elle peult, la garda
> pour quelque temps de monstrer sa volunté. Si est-ce que à la fin la

[47] *Ibid.*, p. 132.
[48] *Ibid.*, p. 132.
[49] *Ibid.*, p. 132.
[50] Novella 18, p. 138.

forteresse du cueur où l'honneur demeure, fut ruynée de telle
sorte que la pauvre dame s'accorda ce dont elle n'avoit poinct esté
discordante.[51]

Even though she has decided finally to give in to the young
gentleman student's desire, she, like the Milanese widow, tests
him. First she has him lie all night in the same bed with her and
ask for nothing more than a kiss. Then she asks him to address his
attentions to a younger, prettier girl, finally substituting this girl
for herself after arranging an assignation in her bedroom. His love
proves sufficiently strong to obey her commands and resist the
temptations set in his path even if, ironically enough, it is the
lady who, after the first test, is "plus esmerveillée que contente."[52]
But her lover is investing in the future by forgoing immediate
satisfaction for the sake of subsequently richer enjoyment; as the
narrator explains, "Amour, qui jamais n'est sans esperance,
l'asseura que plus la fermeté de son amour estoit grande et
congneue par tant d'experience, plus la joissance en seroit longue
et heureuse."[53] And he proves to be right, for the lady apologizes
for the pain she has inflicted on him and rewards him with the
fruition of his love, "telle qu'il la povoit desirer."[54]

This story is interesting because of the insight it gives into
Marguerite's conception of a love which, while morally questionable, is still worthy of admiration. It is by way of being her definition
of 'mixed' love, which like 'pure' love hinges on the genuineness
and exclusiveness of the lovers' attachment. The young lover is not
motivated only by physical desire, although his objective is unquestionably the full possession of the lady. He wishes to have her
only when he has convinced her that he is worthy of her, and he
consequently curbs his natural drives for the sake of his ideal of a
spiritual as well as physical communion with the beloved. That is
why he is infuriated when he discovers the substitution of the young
girl for the woman he expected to make love to – he feels it as an
insult to the sincerity of his desire. The satisfactions he seeks are

[51] *Ibid.*, p. 138.   [52] *Ibid.*, p. 139.   [53] *Ibid.*, p. 140.   [54] *Ibid.*, p. 140.

those of a full-fledged relationship with the woman he loves, and, interestingly enough, his is one of the very few stories in the *Heptameron* with a happy ending; it would seem that where love is natural and proposes a reasonable goal, it may yet lead to temporal happiness. Here again, however, the story offers no assurance of the permanence of this relationship; it is content to sketch the portrait of a perfect lover and indicate the nature of the satisfaction that can be his.

If one of the considerations in love affairs is the honor of the lady, the sexual aggressiveness of the man is obviously important too. The pattern of aggressiveness civilized but not squelched by courtly manners these two tales of successful love present is even more tellingly depicted in the story of Bonnivet and the Italian lady whom he conquers through cleverness. The hero, again, is a model Renaissance courtier who readily becomes a favorite of Milanese society "tant pour sa beaulté, bonne grace et bonne parole, que pour le bruict que chascun luy donnoit d'estre ung des plus adroitz et hardyz aux armes qui fust poinct de son temps."[55] He has occasion to make use of his 'goodly speech' when he meets an attractive woman at a dance; he plies her with the "propos d'amour qu'il sçavoit mieulx que nul autre dire,"[56] and although she turns him down, declaring herself not interested in love, he pursues her, "veu la mauvaise grace que son mary avoit et la grande beaulté d'elle."[57] She is a *mal mariée*, he has decided, and cannot therefore remain indifferent to love, and, surely enough, when he makes inquiries, he discovers that she loves an Italian gentleman "bien saige et honneste." He sets about his campaign to win the lady. First he befriends her Italian lover and so wins his confidence that he is entrusted with the guidance of their love affair. He maneuvers his newfound friend into getting an assignation in the lady's bedroom where, she promises, she will give herself to

---

[55] Novella 14, pp. 109-110. These are practically the same terms as those applied to the hero of the sixteenth tale.
[56] *Ibid.*, p. 110.
[57] *Ibid.*, p. 110.

him. Bonnivet then has his hair and beard styled like the Italian's and takes his place in the lady's bed, revealing his identity only after he has taken possession of and satisfied her. Having thus avenged himself on her coldness towards him, he calms her anger by convincing her that his was the greater and more secret love and that, therefore, he was the more dependable lover; finally, as he leaves to make room for his rival, "la rendit si satisfaicte qu'elle eust bien voulu qu'il y fust demoré plus longuement."[58] When the unfortunate Italian arrives, she dismisses him, pretending to be ill and full of remorse at having agreed to an illicit affair, and from then on restricts herself to Bonnivet, whose love lasts, according to the narrator, "comme la beaulté des fleurs des champs."[59]

Two patterns are discernible in this story. There is the courtly pattern: the lady is a *mal mariée;* her lover first sets eyes on her at a public assemblage; he himself has the appearance and manners of a courtly lover; and he emulates his rival in order to prove himself worthier of her love. But this pattern is only a surface coating of good manners spread over the underlying design of the joke perpetrated on a woman by an aggressively enterprising male. Not only is the lady not idealized, she is proved a fool for believing Bonnivet's declarations and for giving in so readily to sensual gratification. The story is a clear case of the battle of the sexes: masculine superiority has been established in the woman's ready acquiescence to the sexual pleasure imposed on her by force, and the man's wish to assert his greater strength is expressed in his desire, when in bed with the lady, to take her honor and chastity "sans luy en sçavoir gré ni grace"[60] – a desire which bespeaks more hostility than love. The courtly myth is exploded: she is a fool while he is a deceiver, and although the joke is on her, she has at least had her share of the enjoyment. But by founding their relationship exclusively in physical possession, they prevent it from penetrating important areas of their lives and limit its

[58] *Ibid.*, p. 113.    [59] *Ibid.*, p. 114.    [60] *Ibid.*, p. 112.

duration. This and the two stories previously discussed suggest an interesting comparison. Where the relationship is most idealistic the future is not mentioned. Where it is still intensely personal, though less perfect, there is a hint of the impossibility of permanence. And where it is most sensual and warlike, we are told it will last only a season. The more you build on the flesh, the more impermanent the structure you have devised – this seems to be Marguerite's moral. It also follows that the less lovers invest of themselves in a love relationship, the lower their position on the ladder of love.

If Bonnivet's dalliance mocks the possibility of a valid emotional relationship, the purely sensual self-indulgence described in several other novellas does so even more. In the third, for instance, we see the happy arrangement worked out at the court of Naples: the King shares the favors of a courtier's wife while the Queen bestows hers on the betrayed husband. Here lust and the desire for vengeance have disguised themselves as love as both the King and his courtier assume the pose of courtly lovers. The monarch, foreseeing the difficulty of winning the lady because of the great love that bound her to her husband, kept his passion secret for a long time, and sought solace in festivities to which the lady and her husband were faithfully invited. He suspects that it is only the husband's presence that stands in the way of his love, and having sent him away on business, finds that, much more concerned with her honor than her conscience, the lady easily forgets her husband's love. The courtier in turn is motivated solely by revenge when he addresses himself to the Queen; yet he, too, plays the role of the impassioned lover: he urges the Queen to avenge herself, but mid-way in his argument suddenly ascribes his motive to the burning passion consuming his heart – "Revenchons-nous, ma dame, non tant pour leur rendre ce qu'ilz meritent, que pour satisfere à l'amour qui, de mon costé, ne se peult plus porter sans morir."[61] So much for the great love which was supposed to

[61] Novella 3, p. 25.

bind husband and wife together! The Queen, so moved by this declaration that she cannot speak, drifts with her newly found suitor to an even more isolated part of the garden in which they have been conversing, and there they "jouerent la vengeance dont la passion avoit esté importable."[62] The deal becomes permanent, and the gentleman joins the Queen whenever the King seeks the lady's company, so that they are always four "participans au plaisir que deux cuydoient avoir tous seuls."[63] The basis of the pleasure, however, seems to lie more in the delight of deceiving deceivers than in sensual gratification, and so cynical a story is not made less so by the fact that this is one of the few arrangements that last until the participants reach old age.

Cynical indulgence and aggressiveness are not, of course, the exclusive prerogative of men, and the *Heptameron* contains several tales centered on the deceitful incontinence of women. The outstanding hypocrite in this gallery of concupiscent women is a court lady named Jambicque, the heroine of the forty-third novella. Like other women of the court, she is very much concerned with safeguarding her honor and reputation, so much so that she trusts no man with her love. She has fallen in love, though, but is too proud to reveal her plight by look or word, and therefore keeps her feelings locked within herself for more than a year until she can no longer bear the strain. Determined to seek what the narrator terms "le dernier remede," but having concluded that "il valloit mieulx satisfaire à son desir et qu'il n'y eust que Dieu seul qui congneut son cueur, que de le dire à ung homme qui le povoit reveler quelquefois,"[64] she decides to give herself to the man she loves without revealing her identity, thus insuring the safety of her reputation. She offers herself to her chosen lover in the dark seclusion of a deserted gallery on condition that he be willing to meet her only in the dark and that he agree never to try to discover her identity. He agrees and gains possession fairly quickly, for his acquiescence "la rendit très facile à luy rendre la

---

[62] *Ibid.*, p. 26.      [63] *Ibid.*, p. 26.      [64] Novella 43, p. 297.

pareille: c'est de ne luy refuser chose qu'il voulsist prendre."[65]
Understandably, under such circumstances the only contact
possible is sexual, and the pride of conquest takes precedence over
what might otherwise be the romantic lure of an unknown
mistress – the fact of Jambicque's high social rank, revealed to his
touch by the material of her dress, seems to determine the lover's
behavior:

> L'heure estoit de cinq et six en yver, qui entierement lui ostoit la
> veue d'elle. En touchant ses habillemens, trouva qu'ilz estoient de
> veloux, qui en ce temps-là ne se portoit à tous les jours, sinon par
> les femmes de grande maison et d'auctorité. En touchant ce qui es-
> toit dessoubz autant qu'il en povoit prendre jugement par la main,
> ne trouva rien qui ne fust en très bon estat, nect, et en bon poinct.
> Si mist peine de luy faire la meilleure chere qu'il luy fust possible.
> De son costé, elle n'en feit moins. Et congneut bien le gentil homme
> qu'elle estoit mariée.[66]

His curiosity, however, will not let him rest; he has a natural
enough desire to know who the woman is to whom he has been
making love since neither his ego nor his sensibility can derive any
gratification from the completely physical and utterly impersonal
nature of their affair. He discovers her identity by marking her
back with a piece of chalk. Having learned, to his amazement,
that his mistress is none other than the haughtily prudish Jambicque, he woos her openly, but to his surprise she dismisses his suit
with angry contempt, and when he finally confronts her with the
evidence, she brazens it out, accusing him of slander, and has him
exiled from court for his behavior. We may dismiss Jambicque
as a viciously hypocritical woman, but what is significant about
her conduct is its attempt to make the best of two worlds; yet,
in trying to eat her cake and have it, too, she can have neither.
She corrupts the meaning of honor – thereby vitiating the social
code, and excludes from love the personal intimacy which is at
the heart of any romantic attachment. It is her wish to keep her

[65] *Ibid.*, pp. 297-298.     [66] *Ibid.*, p. 298.

93

reputation intact that has led her to become the aggressor; in psychological terms, she plays both masculine and feminine roles, and it is her cold-blooded self-centeredness which shocks. The point is made by Parlamente's comment in the discussion that "celles qui sont vaincues en plaisir ne se doibvent plus nommer femmes, mais hommes, desquelz la fureur et la concupiscence augmente leur honneur."[67]

Other tales in the *Heptameron* treat the concupiscent nature of women, a standard theme of the novella, humorously; still others underline its destructive and tragic consequences. The forty-ninth tale, a light-hearted anecdote, tells of a promiscuous foreign countess, mistress of the French king, who dispenses her favors to six friends, all gentlemen in attendance at court. It is true that she takes her lovers one week at a time, yet, although each knows she is betraying the king, they become indignant when they discover that she is also deceitful to them. Their pride hurt because they have been made sport of, they seek to avenge themselves by shaming her publicy. It is to no avail, however, for she, "qui preferoit son plaisir à tout l'honneur du monde, ne leur en feit pire visaige, ny ne changea de contenance: dont ilz furent tant estonnez, qu'ilz rapporterent en leur saing la honte qu'ilz luy avoient voulu faire."[68] In the final analysis the joke is still on them, and the consequence of feminine prurience is nothing worse than a morally disagreeable situation. The situation is humorous to the extent that six gay blades, who cannot keep a secret and must boast of their good fortune, find themselves outwitted by a clever lady whose moral character is really no worse than theirs.

Social embarrassment and good-hearted humor are the ingredients of several other tales, for instance the anecdote reporting the accidental discovery by Jeanne d'Albret and her husband of the illicit loves of a provincial lady and a protonotary,[69] or the story of the supposedly haunted house from which the servants kept the owner so that they might freely indulge their erotic desires.[70]

[67] *Ibid.*, disc., p. 301.
[68] Novella 49, pp. 321-322.
[69] Novella 66.
[70] Novella 39.

But a woman's indulgence of her sexual impulses can lead to disastrous results, and it is perhaps significant that the *Heptameron* should open with one such story, a true story substantiated by contemporary documents uncovered by Le Roux de Lincy in the French National Archives.[71] The plot, somewhat involved, is actuated by the prurience and greed of an attorney's wife who, having submitted to the desires of the local bishop out of mercenary considerations, has afterwards taken a younger lover for pleasure. When the young man, having discovered her double-dealing, refuses to have anything further to do with her, she is so angry that she plots his destruction. She pretends to her husband that he has been trying to force her to his love and, having lured him to a secret meeting in her house, has her husband arrange his assassination. But her taste for violence has only been stimulated. When she discovers that her husband is trying to kill her through necromancy, she has him arrested and sent to the galleys for that very crime, and revels in her freedom to be evil. One is a little surprised at the abruptly moral conclusion: "La mauvaise femme, en l'absence de son mary, continua son peché plus que jamais et mourut miserablement."[72] Hers is undoubtedly an un-Christian death which leads to punishment in the afterlife, but the statement may be meant, too, as a comment on the quality of her career on earth.

In a similar vein the sixtieth and sixty-first novellas trace the stories of two wives whose willful lust leads them to abandon their husbands by feigning death in order that they might live with their lovers. In each case the husband is ultimately forced to take back his wife. The situation is especially painful for the husband of the sixtieth story, for he has remarried in the meantime, but it is in the sixty-first that the character of the wife is fully developed. Her remarkable will power and determination are presented as the results of lust and perverseness – the story insists on this perverseness, terming hers a 'folle' and 'meschante amour,' yet her love

71 See *L'Heptaméron*, p. 451, n. 75.
72 Novella 1, p. 17.

for a canon leads to what is seemingly a true marriage relationship. The lovers live together openly for some fourteen-odd years and have children (one daughter even makes a highly advantageous marriage), and the woman takes pride in her household, "car elle avoit changé sa honte en gloire d'estre dame de la maison d'un si riche homme."[73] Her plea to the French Queen, Louise de Savoie, and Marguerite de Navarre, all three of whom wish to break up the illicit *ménage*, deserves a careful hearing because it questions, by implication, the validity of social institutions which stand in the way of the fulfillment of perfectly normal human desires. 'I beg of you,' she tells the three ladies,

> que voulez garder que l'on ne touche poinct à mon honneur, car, Dieu mercy! j'ay vescu avec monsieur le chanoine si bien et si vertueusement, qu'il n'y a personne vivant qui m'en sceut reprendre. Et, s'il ne fault point que l'on pense que je vive contre la volunté de Dieu, car il y a trois ans qu'il ne me fut riens, et vivons aussy chastement et en aussy grande amour, que deux beaulx petits anges, sans que jamais entre nous deux y eut eu parolle ne volunté au contraire. Et, qui nous separera fera grand peché, car le bon homme, qui a bien près de quatre vingtz ans, ne vivra pas longuement sans moy, qui en ay quarante cinq.[74]

It may strike the modern reader as ironic that a relationship appearing so in accord with the Christian ideal of marriage should be the product of an illicit *liaison* which contravenes every moral and religious tenet institutionalized by society. For Marguerite, however, the irony must have resided in the fact that so depraved a woman should speak in such noble terms of a passion which cannot be condoned. The woman actually justifies her immorality in the name of the very ethics her behavior has confounded! Such a perversion of values cannot be tolerated, and the union is consequently broken up by none others than Marguerite herself, her mother, and her sister-in-law. And the rightness of their decision is indicated when, faced with the inevitable, the woman repents, "mercyant les dames de ce qu'elles luy avoient gecté

[73] Novella 61, p. 375.    [74] *Ibid.*, p. 375.

ung diable de dessus les espaulles."[75] Here again the erotic and affective impulses in man have brought about a set of circumstances which, if universalized, would be destructive to the social fabric. If the individuals concerned do not have the proper restraints within themselves, society must intervene and curb them; in either case control must exist, even at the expense of the lovers' happiness.

The total perversion of social, moral, and even psychological standards brought about by the weakness of a terribly foolish woman is illustrated in Marguerite's rendering of the incest tale which appears in countless *novellieri*,[76] and which Marguerite picks up in its medieval version of double incest involving first mother and son, and then the son and his daughter-sister. It is the use to which she puts the well-known story-pattern that is of interest, for, stripping it of its mythic and legendary overtones to present it as a factual account of a series of unfortunate events, she underlines the sheer folly of a mother's pride that challenges the deeply rooted natural impulses of the flesh.

A young widow, mother of an only son, has decided never to remarry and has, instead, become devout to the point of denying the existence of the world, "fuyant entierement toutes compaignies de mondanité, tellement qu'elle faisoit conscience d'assister à nopces ou d'ouyr sonner les orgues en une eglise."[77] Blind to the changes wrought in her fourteen-year-old son by Nature — "qui est maistre d'escolle bien secret,"[78] she is shocked to discover that the boy has been pursuing one of her attendant ladies. She refuses to believe that he actually wishes to do something improper and decides to see for herself by taking that lady's place in bed on the night the boy is to join her. Proud of her moral righteousness and her ability to control the situation, she permits the inevitable to

[75] *Ibid.*, p. 376.
[76] See *L'Heptaméron*, Le Roux de Lincy et Anatole de Montaiglon, eds. (Paris, 1880) IV, 281 ff. for a list of such tales.
[77] Novella 30, p. 229.
[78] *Ibid.*, p. 230.

happen: as the narrator puts it, "sa patience fut si longue et sa nature si fragille, qu'elle convertit sa collere en ung plaisir trop abominable, obliant le nom de mere."[79] Naturally deeply perturbed by the unforeseen turn of events, she fails to learn the lesson that the flesh, unaided by God, can turn only to sin; concerned only with arranging matters so as to avoid a repetition of the incest, she decides to send her son away. She then gives birth in secret to a girl whom she consigns to her brother for her upbringing, and spends the rest of her days in fasts and mourning. Her punishment, however, has not ended, for her son eventually marries the girl and brings her home, and the unfortunate woman is daily subjected to the torture of witnessing demonstrations of the love binding her two children. Even her confession to the Legate of Avignon is to no avail, for he declares the children innocent and enjoins complete and absolute silence on her.

This tale exemplifies the tragic disorder that can ensue from the weakness of the flesh left to its own devices, when natural instinct is not properly integrated into a sanely balanced life and controlled by an enlightened spirit. Hircan, the narrator, leaves no doubt about the cause of the mother's dizzying fall: she had, for years, imposed unnatural restraints upon herself and, "tout ainsy que l'eaue par force retenue court avecq plus d'impetuosité quant on la laisse aller, que celle qui court ordinairement, ainsy ceste pauvre dame tourna sa gloire à la contrainte qu'elle donnoit à son corps."[80] The unfortunate but not altogether unpredictable result was that "quant elle vint à descendre le premier degré de son honnesteté, se trouva soubdainement portée jusques au dernier."[81] Marguerite wishes her readers to know that an unnatural constraint can be as disastrous in its consequences as reckless abandon to one's lust. She does not advocate giving in to all one's impulses; she does, however, seem to believe in self-control rather than repression. After all, with all due consideration to the difference in degree, the case of the incestuous mother does not differ in kind

---

[79] *Ibid.*, p. 230.    [80] *Ibid.*, p. 230.    [81] *Ibid.*, pp. 230-231.

from that of Jambicque, who had also cut herself off from all normal outlets for her amatory impulses and was consequently reduced to seeking the 'last remedy' from the very start.

Where, on the other hand, chastity is the natural consequence of a woman's self-respect, the Queen of Navarre can only applaud, and she provides her audience with several examples. The nun Marie Héroet resists the blandishments, threats, and punitive measures of the prior of St. Martin des Champs, who wishes to seduce her.[82] Her behavior is what is to be expected of a nun, and is exceptional only in the light of the fact that hers is the only instance in the *Heptameron* of a truly chaste nun. Self-respect also motivates the heroine of the fourth novella, believed to be none other than Marguerite herself.[83] The lady, sister of a prince of Flanders, spends the night at the home of one of her brother's vassals, a man who, having introduced himself into her bedchamber through a secret passageway, tries to take her by surprise. She, however, fights back vigorously, scratching the poor lover's face so thoroughly that he is forced to make a hasty retreat and does not dare show himself on the morrow for fear of being recognized.

The second novella presents the touching story of a muleteer's wife who chooses to die rather than give in to the lewd desires of a lowly servant, and the fifth tells the tale of an equally lowly ferrywoman who outwits two lascivious monks. These stories in praise of women who value themselves sufficiently to resist at any cost the attacks of men bent on the satisfaction of their lust stand as correctives to those stories depicting the moral laxity of women.[84] They are designed as a perpetual warning against men's intentions and serve as a reminder of the dangers besetting those who enter upon the paths of love – a point explicitly set forth in the story of the princess of Flanders by her lady-in-waiting, who delivers a brief homily against the treacherous snares of love:

[82] Novella 22.
[83] See *L'Heptaméron*, p. 453, n. 125.
[84] Novella 4 contrasts with Novella 62, for instance.

Et devez plus que jamais craindre de recepvoir propos d'amityé, pource qu'il y en a assez qui sont tombez la seconde fois aux dangiers qu'elles ont evité la premiere. Ayez memoire, ma dame, que l'Amour est aveugle, lequel aveuglit de sorte que, où l'on pense le chemyn plus seur, c'est à l'heure qu'il est le plus glissant.[85]

The honor of women is too easily lost to be trifled with, a principle which the Queen of Navarre insists on repeatedly, and both the examples of feminine chastity and the instances of women's incontinence drive the lesson home. It should be noted, however, that the examples of continence described above have nothing whatever to do with the Neoplatonic ladder, for they are predicated on the rejection of sexual love not for the sake of a higher ideal of *love*, but for the sake of social, moral, or religious ideals, a fact which the passage quoted from the officious lady-in-waiting's sermon makes unmistakably clear.

The roll call of concupiscent women has taken us down the ladder of love to a point where the still idealistic 'mixed' love of the troubadours becomes indistinguishable from lust, a condition which precludes the possibility of any kind of real personal relationship. We have already encountered stories in which the motivating principle is the sexual aggressiveness of the male, but in most of these the erotic drive was coupled with some sort of more complete relationship with the love object. The *Heptameron* also contains numerous tales in which immediate gratification of physical desire is the only object in view, an object which leads to brutal assaults that wreak havoc in the lives of the innocent victims. The story of the muleteer's wife is a case in point: the woman is surprised in bed by her servant, who wields a naked sword with which he hopes to frighten her. As she resists him fiercely, he strikes and wounds her so severely that she eventually loses her strength. When she is no longer able to defend herself, he rapes her and makes his escape, leaving her to die. But aside from stories of husbands pursuing their wives' maids – a

[85] Novella 4, p. 32.

theme generally treated in jocular fashion – this is the only story of sexual violence which does not involve members of the clergy; reading the *Heptameron* one might be tempted to conclude that lust is the almost exclusive prerogative of monks and friars.

While it is true that the *Decameron*, the *Cent Nouvelles Nouvelles*, and other such collections provided Marguerite with ample precedents for tales of the scurrility and insatiable lasciviousness of the clergy, it may still come as a surprise to find that the deeply religious Queen of Navarre should have chosen to include in her collection such blatant anticlericalism, especially in the light of her lifelong support of numerous convents and monasteries. One must keep in mind, however, that anticlericalism was also characteristic of evangelical piety in the sixteenth century. Not only did Erasmus reject the monastic ideal as a path for Christian life, he also satirized the mores of the clergy.[86] Others followed suit, but the scorn for monasticism was not restricted to professional humanists and reformers; monks and friars were cordially detested by all enlightened minds of the day, and Louise de Savoie, for instance, could write that "l'an 1522, mon fils et moi... commençames à cognoistre les hypocrites, blancs, noirs, gris, enfumés et de toutes couleurs, desquels Dieu par sa clemence et bonté infinie nous vueille preserver et deffendre; car si Jesus Christ n'est menteur, il n'est pas de plus dangereuse generation en toute nature humaine."[87] This universal dislike was undoubtedly due in great measure to the social and economic parasitism of the monasteries, but there is a particular aspect of the evangelical attacks against monks which is especially revelant to the *Heptameron*: the accusation of unbridled lechery. According to the liberal thinkers of the day, virginity was a special gift of God vouchsafed to only a few; the monastic vows of celibacy and chastity were therefore sheer folly since they imposed an obligation it was not

[86] See Renaudet, *Préréforme*, pp. 387-388; Febvre, *Le Problème de l'incroyance*, p. 335.
[87] Quoted in Mayer, p. 110. Cf. Oisille's "l'ypocrisye de ceulx qui s'estiment plus religieux que les autres," Novella 22, disc., p. 186.

in the power of most men to live up to.[88] Not only that, but by denying members of the clergy an outlet for their normal libidinous desires these vows only encouraged the lechery that was so offensive a part of their behavior. Rabelais had this idea in mind when, in the constitution of Thélème, he allowed those who were so inclined to leave the abbey in order to marry; Marot, in his *Second Chant de l'Amour fugitif*, echoed the same thought when he declared that the vow of chastity went against nature and hinted that monkish lasciviousness was a kind of revenge on the part of Venus against those who would despise her.[89]

Marguerite, for her part, remained true to Fabrist thought and was not ready to reject monasticism *in toto*. Nonetheless, she was familiar with the arguments against it,[90] and she certainly shared the humanists' contempt for the practices of monks and friars, since she chose to ascribe most of her examples of lust to them. Her examples, however, do not necessarily lead to the conclusion that monasticism must be abolished; at most they indicate the pressing need for reform.

Even though her anticlerical salvos were in keeping with the evangelical movement to which she subscribed, one may still wonder why Marguerite decided to include them in a work devoted to a discussion of love. To dismiss the question by saying that the material was traditional will not do. But if one remembers that the disgraceful behavior of monks was an important issue in Marguerite's day, and if one further notes that, with one or two exceptions, her examples of monkish depravity are limited to uncontrolled sexual appetite, the relevance of this material to the over-all design of the *Heptameron* becomes apparent: lust is destructive of the moral order on which Christian society rests. What better demonstration of the hideousness of the sin could there be than the attribution of sexual violence to the very

---

[88] See M. A. Screech, *The Rabelaisian Marriage* (London, 1958) pp. 69-70.
[89] On Rabelais, see Screech, p. 29; on Marot, Mayer, p. 111.
[90] Marguerite had Luther's *De votis monasticis* translated into French. See Mayer, p. 111, n. 37.

members of society whose vocation should most remove them from the stings of lust? Rape, after all, is bad enough in itself, but when, as in the forty-sixth story, it is perpetrated by a friar invited by a mother to remonstrate with her daughter for her laziness, we feel that it is not just an unfortunate accident, but the violation of an important principle of moral and social order as well. In either case the girl's integrity as a free individual would have been violated, but the shattering of a trust on which mankind should be able to rely makes the crime all the more disquieting.

Two other examples will show the extent of Marguerite's concern over the anarchy resulting from the betrayal of clerical ideals. The twenty-third novella relates the subterfuge of a Franciscan monk who gains possession of the lady of the house where he has been received as a guest. He substitutes himself for her husband in bed and then leaves before the husband is due to come to her. The couple discover the trick that has been played on them, and the husband sets off in pursuit of the offender. In the meantime the lady, "non seullement divertye de l'espoir que tout chrestien doibt avoir en Dieu, mais ... du tout allienée du sens commung, obliant sa propre nature,"[91] strangles herself and in the process accidentally kills her new-born son. At this juncture her brother appears on the scene and, suspecting the husband, chases after him and kills him in a duel. A whole family has been wiped out, but the friar responsible goes uncaught and unpunished.

In the thirty-first story, a friar who has fallen in love with the wife of a nobleman loses all command of his rational faculties. He takes advantage of the husband's absence from home one day to dispatch the servants with his dagger and force the frightened woman to cut her hair and don the dress of a novice so that he may safely abduct her to his monastery. The husband happens to meet them on the way but does not recognize his wife, who is too frightened by her abductor's dagger to reveal her identity; his servant, however, has recognized his mistress and follows after them, only

91 Novella 23, p. 191.

to be killed by the friar. The husband, alerted, rushes to the scene and overcomes the cleric's resistance; he forces a confession from him and leads him, a prisoner, to judgment at the Emperor's court. There it becomes known that many gentlewomen have been so abducted, and, the prisoners having been released from the monastery, it is burned to the ground with all its members inside. This punishment is intended as a perpetual reminder of the crimes perpetrated there, and the lesson the story teaches, the narrator concludes, is that "il n'y a rien plus dangereux qu'amour, quant il est fondé sur vice, comme il n'est rien plus humain ne louable, que quant il habite en ung cueur vertueulx."[92]

Although Marguerite here substitutes the Christian ideal of virtue for the courtly doctrine of the gentle heart, she, too, is expressing the idea that it is not so much the act of love in itself that matters as the psychological circumstances surrounding it. Like the Neoplatonists she sees desire as a powerful daemon whose demands cannot be resisted, and her stories are replete with references to the ineluctable power of love; but where Ficino saw embroilment in lust as a case of arrested development, undoubtedly due to the dimmed spiritual vision of the soul occasioned by the Fall, she appears to see it as the deliberate perversion of a soul bent on falling even further from divine grace. Whereas the Neoplatonists cannot admit that this daemon can be a force for evil, with Marguerite love can work for good or evil according to the spiritual state of the person it acts upon. We have seen many instances of its destructive impact, but we should be careful to note that this impact is conditioned not only by the avowed goal of the lover but also by the situation into which he introduces his desire. The story of the deceitful friar, for instance, depends entirely on devices of deceit and substitution which appear in many other stories where they do not entail such catastrophic consequences. Similarly, the rape of the muleteer's wife in the second story leads to her death, but the heroine of the sixty-second story, who is also

92 Novella 31, p. 240.

taken by force, readily accommodates herself to the situation and even boasts of her adventure to a royal princess, who (it has been conjectured) may be Marguerite herself.

Why, then, is one lover lewd and rapacious while the other is gallant and adventurous? Why should the story of the monk who pre-empts the bridegroom's function on his wedding night produce laughter[93] when a like action by the Franciscan friar arouses indignation? The answer is that in the *Heptameron* love is not just the desire of the lover for the love-object but manifests itself as interaction between two persons and often involves others as well. Where the *fait accompli* is readily accepted, no great suffering ensues; but where no such predisposition exists the resultant situation causes unbearable pain to the victims and borders on tragedy. The heroine of the sixty-second story is a *mal mariée*; the bride of the forty-eighth only loses her virginity; the Milanese lady surprised by Bonnivet[94] actually admires him for his boldness and comes to prefer him to her Italian suitor — in none of these cases is any great harm done. The muleteer's wife, on the other hand, is thoroughly horrified by her servant's demands and cannot choose but resist even if she must die; and it is interesting to speculate on what would have resulted had the attempted rape of the princess of Flanders been successful. As for the friar's victim in the twenty-third novella, the deceit perpetrated on her and her husband appears as an uneradicable stain corrupting the harmony of a happy marriage into which an heir has just been born. The friar's crime is heinous not only because he has grossly abused the hospitality of his hosts, but also because he has knowingly and willingly spoiled something truly beautiful: a happy, healthy union between two people who love one another. It is this spoliation that the victim cannot live with, and here the daemon of love has showered disaster on man because it came to a heart dedicated to vice; a virtuous heart, however much it might falter at times, would not have injected itself into this situation.

[93] Novella 48.          [94] See above, pp. 89 ff.

With these stories we have descended to a level well beneath the point where the Neoplatonic *scala d'amore* begins to rise; we are in the realm of Ficino's physical 'furor' which reduces man to the level of an animal and leads him nowhere,[95] and the action of the daemon that is love has been shown to be well-nigh universal. There would seem to be, then, nothing more to be said on the subject. But as Marguerite is embarked on a moral inquiry which embraces the psychological and social relationships which devolve from love, and since her approach is by way of the contacts established between the sexes, she must of necessity take into consideration the one institution by means of which society has sought to regulate and regularize the commerce between men and women, marriage.

The *Heptameron* illustrates, therefore, different kinds of marital relationships. Much of the material is conventional in that it follows the *fabliau* tradition of laughing at wedlock as a form of mutual enslavement from which each partner seeks to escape. But considering the vast number of such tales of deceiving husbands and outwitting wives extant in the literature of her time, Marguerite's contribution to the *genre* is relatively slight, and her examples usually serve to point a moral. There is a scale of values by which the behavior of husbands and wives is to be judged. It is not identical with the traditional ladder of love since the latter was devised to deal with extra- or nonmarital relationships; it runs parallel to it, however, in the sense that the values of faithfulness and true affection are idealized and placed at the top whereas debauchery is relegated to the bottom. The twenty-third story, for instance, the story of the tragedy wrought by the Franciscan's lust, offers a thumbnail sketch of a happy marriage in which the bonds of mutual affection have been strengthened by the arrival of a son – in the words of the narrator, "la femme dudict gentil homme, qui estoit belle et non moins saige et vertueuse, avoit faict ung beau filz dont l'amityé que le mary luy portoit augmenta

[95] See above, p. 44.

doublement."[96]  Not only is the husband happy with his wife, but he also is apparently content to center his erotic life in his relationship with her, and the abstinence imposed on him by her pregnancy and lying-in has only made him impatient to resume sexual intimacy. This idyllic picture of wedded bliss, so soon to be shattered by the machinations of the prurient friar, stands in sharp contrast to the many instances of philandering husbands and unfaithful wives which appear in other stories. Marguerite knows that marriage vows are often taken all too lightly and easily broken, but while she can readily see the humor of many an adulterous situation, she refuses to condone it and reserves her praise for those spouses who keep faith with their troth.[97]

Not content merely to condemn extra-marital relations, Marguerite studies the ways in which different people deal with amorous desires that go counter to their marriage vows. The hero of the sixty-third novella, for instance, has accommodated his commitment to the social and economic considerations which require that a man marry and have a family, with the purely private aspirations of his psyche that demand fulfillment in a romantic love relationship. By splitting his affective life in two, he has complemented the pragmatically affectionate relationship subsisting between him and his wife with an equally sincere Platonic attachment to another lady: Dagoucin, the narrator, tells his listeners that his hero

> avoit une femme qui luy portoit de beaulx enfans dont il se contentoit très fort, et vivoient en telle paix que pour rien il n'eut voulu qu'elle eut prins mauvais soupson de luy; d'autre part, il estoit serviteur d'une des plus belles dames qui fut de son temps en France, laquelle il aymoit, estimoit tant, que toutes les aultres luy sembloient laydes auprès d'elle; de sorte que, au commencement de sa jeunesse, et avant qu'il fut marié, n'estoit possible de luy faire veoir ne hanter aultres femmes, quelque beaulté qu'elles eussent; et prenoit plus de plaisir à veoir s'amye et de l'aymer parfaictement que de tout ce qu'il sceut avoir d'une aultre.[98]

[96] Novella 23, p. 187.      [97] Novellas 45, 54, 68, 69, and 71.
[98] Novella 63, p. 380.

Neither half interferes with the other since each involves a separate area of his being, and both are based on the assurance of sexual fidelity to his marriage and spiritual fidelity to his romantic ideal. This assurance is tested when the king asks him to join in an amorous adventure, and we are given further insight into the cordial nature of the hero's relationship with his wife when we find that it is to her he turns for advice on how best to circumvent the king's wish without incurring his wrath.

'Pure' love works in this instance because of the trust and respect husband and wife freely give one another, a trust which presupposes a high degree of maturity on both parts. Where there is no such maturity, neither trust nor happiness can survive. Such would seem to be the lesson of the forty-seventh story, where Marguerite once again turns conventional material to her purpose. The story concerns two young men devoted in friendship since earliest infancy, one of whom has married yet seeks to maintain the total and absolute intimacy of the friendship:

> L'un des deux se maria; toutefois, pour cela, ne laissa-il à continuer sa bonne amityé et tousjours vivre, avecq son bon compaignon, comme il avoit accoustumé; et, quant ilz estoient en quelque logis estroict, ne laissoit à le faire coucher avecq sa femme et luy: il est vray qu'il estoit au millieu. Leurs biens estoient tous en commung, en sorte que, pour le mariage ne cas qui peut advenir, ne sceut empescher ceste parfaicte amityé....[99]

The ideal of heroic friendship that lies at the heart of the knightly code dates back at least to Homer's celebration of Achilles' love for Patroclus. Since its psychological basis is the total identification with the friend, who assumes many of the attributes of a love-object, it leaves no room for heterosexual love; when such love does appear, the two loves come into conflict. Here, however, it is not romantic love that is at issue, but marriage, and the story suggests that a satisfactory marital relationship requires, for the very least, the shedding of pre-adolescent emotional patterns. Not

[99] Novella 47, p. 312.

only does the common sharing of property practiced by the friends violate the economic rationale of marriage, but the sharing of the marriage-bed bespeaks such a strong identification with the friend as an alter ego that the jealousy which besets the hero and destroys both friendship and happy marriage is inevitable. Dagoucin tells the story in order to illustrate the evils of jealousy, and since the discussion follows this path we may safely assume that this is the lesson Marguerite wishes to draw. However, we may also infer that the husband's unreasoned jealousy is a natural consequence of the infantile fantasy he has sought to perpetuate in his relationship with wife and friend. His actions reveal the absence of the maturity which puts one in command of one's self. Without such maturity, a proper relationship is not possible.

Self-respect, self-control, and mutual trust are, in Marguerite's view, the minimal requisites for a good marriage. Three stories of wives who decline the blandishments of love in order to remain true to their vows illustrate this belief. The wife of the twenty-seventh story informs her husband of his friend's amorous designs towards her with the result that the husband is so delighted with her virtue that he feels no concern over his friend's intended dishonesty. In the thirteenth tale, the story of the unhappy captain which we have already seen,[100] the virtuous wife declines the gift of the valuable jewel he sent her and forwards it to *his* wife. In neither of these cases does the chastity of the wife cost her any suffering since neither is in love with her admirer. The twenty-sixth novella, on the other hand, presents a young woman who, although she has all the attributes of the *mal mariée* – a considerably older husband and no children, remains virtuous despite her strong feelings for an attractive young man who has sought to win her love. Her situation is so excruciatingly painful that she eventually pines away and dies. But she has kept faith with her husband's trust, and her self-respect, in keeping unsullied her affection for him, has prevented her marriage from turning to

[100] See above, p. 77.

dross. She has suffered greatly for love; but love, Marguerite would say, is not the necessary foundation for a good relationship between husband and wife: the qualities that make for good companionship are much more important.

When the trust between husband and wife is broken, the consequences will naturally vary with the nature of the people involved. As a rule a wife's infidelity is viewed more seriously than that of a husband – a patrilinear society must of necessity insist on the chastity of the wife in order to insure the purity of genealogical descent – and an outraged husband will exact severe punishment because the honor of his family must be avenged and protected against further stains (thirty-sixth tale) or, and this is more germane to an inquiry into the ways of love, because his great love and trust have turned to fury and despair (thirty-second tale). The problem is more delicate where the wife's lover also happens to be the husband's master or ruler, and the offended husband must often learn to live with a bad situation; he may hope, as in the third story, to avenge his wounded ego by repaying his benefactor in kind.[101] The waywardness of husbands, on the other hand, leaves women small latitude for redress; they must usually suffer in silence and hope to regain their spouses' affections by their patience and indulgence, using their good sense and tact to shame their husbands back to them (thirty-seventh tale), or foolishly seeking the remedy of a love potion (sixty-eighth tale). Some few, however, are not content to remain passive and, like the heroines of the fifteenth and fifty-ninth stories, rebel against the double standard which gives husbands a free hand in the game of love while prohibiting the slightest dalliance to the wives. Here again the breach of trust leads to undesirable consequences: each lady makes her husband's infidelity the occasion of her emancipation from the subordinate position traditionally imposed upon the

---

101 The twelfth novella relates the assasination of Alessandro de'Medici, first duke of Florence, in 1537, by his cousin Lorenzino, and attributes it to the Duke's desire for his cousin's sister. But it is a sister, not a wife, whose honor is being defended.

wife, a rebellion which destroys the proper balance of the marriage. But the interest of these two stories goes beyond the obvious moral that they point: by exhibiting the conflicting desires and needs which frequently oppose husbands and wives, they expose the personal dissatisfaction encountered in marriage and provide a serious critique of the institution.

The cause of dissatisfaction in the fifteenth novella is not hard to find, for it is the story of the traditional *mal mariée* transplanted to the realistic setting of life at court. In it Marguerite combines elements from the *chanson de toile*, the medieval lament of the girl afire with love who cannot overcome the obstacle of her beloved's indifference, with the well-worn pattern of the unhappily married wife who seeks solace for her loveless match to an older, jealous husband in the arms of a younger and more capable lover; but she turns these conventional patterns into a revealing study of aristocratic mores. The marriage which is the subject of the story is a marriage of convenience, arranged by the king to better the fortunes of a favored but impoverished courtier. It is, from the man's point of view, a purely economic arrangement designed for his personal advantage, and he enjoys his wife's wealth without the least regard for any obligation he might have towards her. She is a young, inexperienced girl who holds no interest for him; he disposes of her by placing her in the care of a great lady at court so that he may be free to lead the life of courtier and lover he relishes. His wife, sexually and emotionally starved and deprived of the security of affection and respect a woman requires, eventually turns to a lover for the fulfillment she hoped for from her husband. "In such circumstances a woman might be excused for feeling that love afforded her a certain insurance against the uncertainties of marriage.... The security, spiritual and economic, which the husband did not offer, the wife might well look for in the lover; at least so the matter was rationalized."[102] And it is the lady's challenge of the conventional notions of masculine and feminine

[102] Valency, p. 77.

honor and her assertion of the woman's right to her emotional independence when the man has failed in his duty as husband that holds our attention in this story. Telling her husband that her love for him encountered his scorn from the very beginning, she explains that unhappiness turned her love to hatred, and her desire to obey changed to a desire to avenge herself. The first glimmer of happiness came when a prince fell in love with her, but he shortly abandoned his suit at the king's command. Then she found her present lover who, she claims, "m'a aymée avecq tant d'honnesteté, que oncques en sa vie ne me requist chose que l'honneur ne luy peust accorder."[103] After insisting on the innocence of the pleasure she sought, she comes to her main point, which is that her husband is the one who is really at fault, that, guiltier in his behavior than she, he has no business objecting to her actions. She argues that he alone is responsible for what she still terms her unhappiness; she declares that he set her an example far less honorable than anything she has done, for, she tells him, "vous le sçavez et je sçay bien que celle que vous aymez ne se contente poinct de ce que Dieu et la raison commandent";[104] and she finally challenges the double standard in the name of Christian morality when she adds to her comment about her husband's mistress that "combien que la loy des hommes donne grand deshonneur aux femmes qui ayment autres que leurs mariz, si est-ce que la loy de Dieu n'exempte poinct les mariz qui ayment autres que leurs femmes."[105] What is sauce for the goose should be sauce for the gander, but she actually uses this argument to justify *her* freedom of action, not to restrict her husband's.

This declaration of feminine independence is also taken up by the lady of the fifty-ninth story, who uses the discovery of her husband's pursuit of a domestic as a weapon in her struggle for freedom of action. Here, interestingly enough, we are dealing with a love match – "par grande amityé de l'ung et de l'autre, se feit le mariage."[106] The lady has admirers – a fact which she

103 Novella 15, p. 122.
104 *Ibid.*, p. 123.
105 *Ibid.*, p. 123.
106 Novella 59, p. 360.

does not hide from her husband, and both find it amusing to watch the game of courtly love. The husband finally tires of both her suitors and her extravagance, objecting to her extended attentions to others than relatives and friends. Furthermore, she spends all her money on clothes, and her husband complains – the scene is familiar enough, as is the subsequent scene in which, having caught her husband in the far more serious act of trying to seduce one of her maids, she uses the moral advantage thus gained to exact his promise to indulge her her harmless pleasures. As he really loves his wife he is truly contrite and agrees to her conditions; but such a conclusion is possible only where the relationship between husband and wife is practically that of equals. The basis of this relationship is, once again, mutual trust – a fact attested to by the wife's openness about her admirers, her keen disappointment at the discovery of her husband's intended infidelity, and her enunciation of a principle concerning the safety of a married woman's honor: a couple's known mutual love and trust is sufficient guarantee for her honor and reputation in the world.[107]

The problems of marriage are not limited, however, to the difficulties encountered when the private desires of the partners clash with the expectations they have of one another. Since unions were arranged on the basis of social and economic considerations which did not necessarily concern themselves with the wishes of the parties most directly affected, the situation of people who wished to marry for love could be exceedingly painful. The story of Rolandine, the heroine of the twenty-first novella, provides an interesting example of a clandestine marriage and its consequences. A nobleman's daughter, she is still unmarried at thirty because of the indifference of her father and the enmity of the Queen. She finds a lover who is equally unfortunate in that he is the illegitimate scion of a noble family and hence devoid of personal fortune. Not at all handsome, he is unable to make his way at court through the

[107] "Une femme, estant bien aymée de son mary et l'aymant de son costé comme elle faisoit, portoit ung sauf-conduict de parler à tout le monde et n'estre mocquée de nul." *Ibid.*, p. 364.

favor of influential ladies. The Queen, however, forbids their meetings. Forced to meet Rolandine in secret, the suitor proposes marriage with the novel argument that it would perpetuate the courtly love relationship which now binds them together – he will be all the better a husband because their union will be based exclusively on love, and he will remain her lover and servant rather than seek to become her master:

> Dieu vous a donné de grandz biens, et estes en dangier d'en avoir encores plus: si j'estoys si heureux que vous me voulussiez eslire pour mary, je vous serois mary, amy et serviteur toute ma vie; et si vous en prenez ung esgal à vous, chose difficille à trouver, il vouldra estre maistre et regardera plus à voz biens que à vostre personne, et à la beaulté que à la vertu; et, en joyssant de l'usufruict de vostre bien, traictera votre corps autrement qu'il ne le merite. Le desir que j'ay d'avoir ce contentement, et la paour que j'ay que vous n'en ayez poinct avecq ung autre, me font vous supplier que, par un mesme moyen, vous me rendez heureux et vous la plus satisfaicte et la mieux traitée femme qui oncques fut.[108]

It is nonsense to say, as one commentator does, that this is the ideal of the Neoplatonic dream realized in the state of matrimony;[109] if anything, it is the courtly dream of the troubadour that is being transplanted into marriage, all the more so as the lover is the lady's social inferior. Rolandine, since she has been forced out of the mainstream of normal social development, accepts the offer, agreeing to build the marriage on love alone. Clandestine marriages were quite common in the sixteenth century, as the repeated attempts to legislate in this domain show; all that was required for the marriage to be valid in the eyes of canon law was an exchange of vows in the presence of a cleric and consummation. In these cases of romantic love put into action, the individual revolted against the oppressive force of the social code. But Rolandine bows to both the social code and the requirements of *fin amor* by insisting that the consummation be put off until such time as she can obtain her father's consent, or

[108] Novella 21, pp. 161-162.    [109] Telle, p. 115.

114

until after his death. Therefore, "se donnerent chascun ung anneau en nom de mariaige, et se baiserent en l'eglise devant Dieu, qu'ilz prindrent en tesmoing de leur promesse; et jamays depuis n'y eut entre eulx plus grande privaulté que de baiser."[110]

The outcome of this clandestine marriage is not altogether happy, for the father, considerably angered by his daughter's action, imprisons her in a castle and refuses to have any dealings with her until she gives up her husband. The husband, for his part, is forced to flee to Germany, where he reveals his true colors by wooing a German lady for her wealth, showing, according to the narrator, that "vraye et parfaicte amour ne luy avoit pas tant faict pour-chasser Rolandine que l'avarice et l'ambition."[111] The social and economic facts of life are too strong for him to remain a romantic lover within a marriage which, unconsummated, would not even be recognized as valid, and Rolandine is left to sustain by herself the ideal of true love in the face of mounting pressure brought to bear upon her by society. That her unfaiful husband conveniently dies shortly thereafter, enabling her to marry a nobleman from her own house, only demonstrates the insufficiency of romantic love as a basis for what is first and foremost a social institution. The romantic fantasy, which by its nature tends to deny the image of life contained in the social code, is not appropriate to the practical considerations that must operate in the running of a successful marriage; it is therefore an inadequate pattern for a satisfactory relationship between husband and wife.

Rolandine's story has a double edge, however, for while it illustrates the dangers of romantic marriage, it also criticizes a social order in which the legitimate aspirations of individuals are frustrated by pride and avarice. The fortieth story is equally sharp in its criticism; there the sister of Rolandine's father has been denied marriage because her brother wished to keep her with him and avoid the disbursement of a dowry. She has fallen in love with a gentleman retainer of the household and, on the strength of her

110 *Ibid.*, p. 162.          111 *Ibid.*, p. 172.

brother's great liking for him, the two have secretly married. When the brother discovers their union he flies into a rage and has his brother-in-law killed on the spot. Although he subsequently regrets the rashness of his action and proposes other husbands to his sister, she will have nothing further to do with life and spends the remainder of her days incarcerated in the castle which will later serve as prison for her niece. The sheer human waste caused by aristocratic pride and selfishness makes the story Marguerite's strongest condemnation of the all-too-common cruelty practiced in disposing of marriageable girls.

The contravening of social dictates and convention is, as we have seen, fraught with danger; but where private wish coincides with social acceptability, there is a chance for happiness. There *is* one example of the they-lived-happily-ever-after type of story in the *Heptameron*, and it concerns two young people who are psychologically and socially suited for one another and who hope to marry.[112] Both members of the middle class – Jacques is the son of a civil servant and Françoise the daughter of a Paris merchant, they eschew the refinements of courtly *fin amor* as their love is presided over not by the Uranian Venus but by her Dionian sister, a fact announced by the narrator, who advises his listeners that love, "au lieu de nous apporter mort, nous rapporte vie, en nous communiquant la propagation des enfans, qui nous rendent immortels; et cela est une des principales causes d'augmenter noz desirs."[113] Jacques presses his suit so eagerly that Françoise is torn

---

[112] Novella II in the Appendix, which appeared as Novella 44 in Gruget's 1559 edition.

[113] Appendix II, p. 433. There may be an echo, here, of Rabelais' view of marriage as a means of perpetuating one's physical and moral self through one's children (Gargantua's letter in *Pantagruel*, VIII; see Screech, pp. 16-22), but the echo is so distant that it seems wiser not to insist on it. It should be noted, however, that ascribing man's immortality to procreation in no way invalidates the concept of the immortality of the soul (see Febvre, *Le Problème de l'incroyance*, pp. 183-225, for a demonstration of this point in connection with Gargantua's letter). Neoplatonism and Evangelical doctrine are here joined in Marguerite's thought.

between the desire to grant him his wish and the fear of giving in, and one day he manages things in such a way that "au lieu de bailler la cotte verte à s'amye, luy bailla la cotte rouge, en sorte que la couleur luy en vint au visaige pour s'estre trouvée surprise un peu plus tost qu'elle ne pensoit."[114] Her regrets and lamentation are quickly stilled by the boy, who leads her back to the meadow, where

> elle ne sceust si bien faire, qu'elle ne receust plus de plaisir à la seconde cotte verte qu'à la premiere: voire et si s'en trouva si bien dès l'heure, qu'ils prindrent deliberation pour adviser comment ils se pourroient reveoir plus souvent et plus à leur aise, en attendant le bon loisir du pere.[115]

The guilt attendant upon this pre-marital consummation is quickly dissipated because they are young, healthy, and know that there can be no reasonable objection to their marriage. They are therefore content to wait and enjoy the full pleasure of their love until such time as her father consents to their wedding. "En quoy," the story concludes,

> ilz ont continué sans scandale... jusques à la consommation du mariage, qui s'est trouvé bien riche pour une fille de marchand, car elle estoit seule. Vray est que Jaques a attendu le meilleur du temporel jusques au decès du pere, qui estoit si serrant qu'il luy sembloit que ce qu'il tenoit en une main l'autre luy desrobboit.[116]

Here, then, is a story of the union of two people based on both love and property values; where the two coincide, a reasonably happy marriage may ensue. Their pre-marital intimacy merely confirms the solidity of their attachment to one another; it is based on something more than a romantic dream, or the fulfillment of desire would have led to the dissolution of their relationship. They discover they are emotionally and sexually right for each

[114] *Ibid.*, p. 436. The expression "bailler la cotte verte," means, in effect, to throw her down on the grass, and "luy bailla la cotte rouge," similarly, means "took her virginity."
[115] *Ibid.*, p. 437.          [116] *Ibid.*, p. 437.

other, and as their marriage makes social and economic sense from the very beginning, they can indeed look forward to living happily ever after. The ideals of *fin amor*, however, have been abandoned in favor of bourgeois notions of romance.

Since the didactic impulse behind the *Heptameron* is very strong, Marguerite could not forgo tracing the education of the lover. Two sets of contrasting stories concerned with this theme deserve to be examined. The tenth and twenty-sixth novellas seem to complement one another, as do the twenty-fifth and forty-second. The twenty-fifth story, the love affair of young Francis I with a certain Parisian lady by name of Mme. Disomme, is very little other than an account of a young man's initiation into active sexual life. It is an amusing anecdote of a young prince who loves the wife of a lawyer and who makes use of a near-by monastery as a short-cut to his lady's domicile and as a cover for his nightly activities – he even stops off to pray on his way back to the palace! His sister, surprised at this sudden spurt of religious piety, learns the truth, but even she is more delighted at her brother's cleverness than shocked by his seeming hypocrisy. It is the representatives of order, civil and spiritual, who are presented as hypocrites, and youth, in the person of the prince, defies and mocks them in the name of the animal vitality he feels rising within him. Besides, as Longarine explains in her lengthy introduction to the story, deception in lovers is laudable and necessary because it is commanded by their tyrannous task-master, love, and, "par ceste nécessité leur est non seullement permis mais mandé de user de mensonge, ypocrisye et fiction, qui sont les moyens de vaincre leurs ennemys, selon la doctrine de maistre Jehan de Mehun."[117] All's fair in love and war; it is the life of the senses that is at issue here, and we can conclude only that the conventions of morality seem paltry when set against the exuberance of youth coming into possession of its powers. Yet even here Marguerite is careful to indicate that the principles of morality are only temporarily set aside, for, Longarine tells us, "combien qu'il menast la vie que je vous diz, si estoit-il

[117] Novella 24, disc., pp. 202-203.

prince craignant et aymant Dieu."[118] The entire story seems to echo Castiglione's assertion that sensual love may be allowed to the young courtier because it is in the nature of youth to feel the compelling force of the senses.[119]

The counterpart to this tale of initiation into the ways of love is the idyllic *pastourelle* which forms the forty-second story, in which a young girl of lowly condition gives a young prince an object lesson in virtue. The prince is probably the young Francis I and the girl, named Françoise, is his first love. Catching sight of her in church one day, he falls in love and pursues her assiduously, thinking that her lowly estate will make her an easy prey. Despite supplications, cajoleries, and threats, she remains adamant in her refusal to part with her honor for his sake, "ne s'estimant digne d'en estre aymée par honneur ou par mariage, ne voulant aussi d'autre part que ce fut par folie et plaisir."[120] Françoise admits her love for the prince, but she will not give in to passion and will therefore not give herself to him because she is "saige et raisonnable." Since the young prince refuses to consider the use of force to bring her to his will, he is left with no alternative but to admire her steadfastness and virtue, which he finally rewards by marrying her to one of his servants. Her example, we are given to understand, has taught him the worth of a woman who has sufficient self-respect to turn down an amorous adventure that can lead her nowhere, even though her feelings are engaged on the side of her suitor.

The tenth story is a long, complex heroic romance told by Parlamente to prove that a woman can be in love and yet remain

---

[118] Novella 25, p. 205. Montaigne, *Essais*, I, 56, is dismayed by Marguerite's approval of her brother's prayer and concludes that "ce n'est pas par cette preuve seulement qu'on pourroit verifier que les femmes ne sont guieres propres à traiter les matieres de la Theologie." *Essais*, Albert Thibaudet, ed. (Paris, 1950) p. 361. He apparently failed to recognize the balance Marguerite was striving for; at any rate, she was certainly not writing as a theologian.
[119] *Cortegiano*, IV, liv.
[120] Novella 42, p. 288.

chaste. The story of the love of Floride and Amadour and of the latter's attempts to achieve the physical consummation of their passion, by the time it comes to a close it has touched on practically all the motifs of the courtly love fantasy: the connection between love and war, the psychological and social relationship of knight to lady, the conflict which opposes love to the social desiderata for marriage, the emergence of sensuality from behind the mask of courtly idealization, the conflict between honor and desire. Amadour, as his name suggests, is a true hero of romance; a handsome nineteen-year-old knight, full of prowess, he has been to school with Castiglione's courtier and is well-spoken, well-mannered, and endowed with unusual good sense. The second son of a rich and honorable family, he is forced to make his way in the world under his own power. He has been favored by Love and Fortune, however, who "delibererent de y faire leur chef d'euvre, et luy donnerent, par le moyen de la vertu, ce que les loys du païs luy refusoient."[121] In traditional fashion, he falls under the spell of the young Floride, loving her at first sight, almost fainting during his first encounter with her, and quickly seeking a screen lady behind whom to hide his true passion. This lady is a wealthy woman who happens to be a member of the household of Floride's mother; he therefore marries her in order to advance his fortunes and secure an entry into the house. He succeeds in gaining the complete confidence of the countess of Arande (Floride's mother) but pushes the disguise of his passion even further by openly wooing another lady. Finally, unable to control the burning fire of his passion any longer, he makes his declaration to Floride in the true tradition of *fin amor*:

> Je ne pretends, pour la fin et recompense de mon service, que une chose: c'est que vous me voulliez estre maistresse si loyalle que jamais vous ne m'esloigniez de vostre bonne grace, que vous me continuiez au degré où je suis, vous fiant en moy plus que en nul aultre, prenant ceste seurté de moy, que, si, pour vostre honneur ou chose qui vous touchast, vous avez besoin de la vie d'un gentil

121 Novella 10, p. 57.

homme, la myenne y sera de très bon cueur employée, et en
pouvez faire estat, pareillement, que toutes les choses honnestes et
vertueuses que je feray seront faictes seullement pour l'amour de
vous.[122]

Amadour is thus the perfect courtier-knight and courtly lover,
whose devotion and loyalty to his lady go so far as to make him
rejoice in her forthcoming marriage to a man she loves. All he asks
is that she accept him as her champion and servant, and remain a
true and loyal mistress to him according to the rules of courtly love.

For her part, Floride is a courtly lady with certain minor modifications: unlike the legion of her sisters, she is barely nubile when
Amadour first loves her (one suspects the influence of the *Vita
Nuova* here) and is therefore unmarried, and, several years later,
she is due to marry some one she loves. But even her impending
marriage does not prevent her from accepting Amadour's services
as a lover, for, as she tells him, "ma conscience ny mon honneur
ne contreviennent poinct à vostre demande, ny l'amour que je
porte au filz de l'Infant Fortuné; car elle est fondée sur mariage,
où vous ne pretendez rien.[123] Marriage and *fin amor* are kept in
separate compartments and do not interfere with one another,
although Floride soon finds that love is a hard master whose fire
robs her of much of her previous equanimity; still, she remains
true to her honor and self-respect as a courtly lady, and strives to
shine in virtue so as to be deemed a worthy mistress for so gallant
a knight as Amadour.

Up to this point Marguerite has unfolded the pattern of an ideal
courtly relationship, the very perfection of which is almost
unbelievable. But while patterns may be static, the experience
which fills them is not, and once action begins to take over in the
romance, the conflicting forces of life proceed to undo the very
pattern which is being imitated. The death of Floride's fiancé
leads her to a loveless match which, in turn, feeds the flames of her
passion for Amadour; the death of Amadour's wife, on the other

[122] *Ibid.*, p. 63.     [123] *Ibid.*, p. 64.

hand, threatens his free access to the countess of Arande's household and provokes him to desperate measures. He attempts to
seduce Floride just as she is about to swear her undying love to him;
she is so shocked and horrified by his behavior that she resolves
never to see him again. Frustrated passion only heightens the
violence of his feelings, however, and he drops all pretence of
courtly propriety when, a few years later, he tries to take her by
force, crying out that since "amour, patience et humble priere ne
servent de riens, je n'espargneray poinct ma force pour acquerir
le bien qui, sans l'avoir, me la feroit perdre."[124] Hatred has
replaced love in his heart, but once again he is foiled by Floride,
and the only recourse left him is death, which he finds on the
battlefield. Floride, widowed by the very same battle which ends
Amadour's life, retires to a convent where she may spend the
remainder of her days in meditation and prayer.

The story of Amadour is fascinating on many counts, not the
least of which is the pattern it traces of moral degeneration from
an ideal. The abstract ideal so readily embraced by Amadour in his
youth crumbles all too easily once the accidents of life threaten to
destroy the carefully erected structure of relationships within
which he thought to live; this structure once laid low, worldly
ambition and sensual desire quite overflow the dam of idealism
which sought to contain them. As we witness the sad spectacle
of the progressive disillusionment of the lovers, we become aware
of the fact that theirs is essentially a negative experience of the
ways of love and that the lesson to be drawn from it requires a
positive counterpart to be complete. The educative experience of
the young seigneur d'Avannes of the twenty-sixth story, whose
contact with two different women gradually changes him from a
callow youth to a man capable of appreciating the value of true
virtue, is its foil; and the key to the difference between the two
stories is to be found in their differing frames of reference, for the
underlying pattern of Amadour's story is derived from the con-

124 *Ibid.*, p. 78.

ventions of the troubadours, whereas the basic design of the other
has an affinity with the stilnovists' concept of true love. Thus the
idealism of the former is confined to the social reality within
which it seeks to operate and is not illuminated by truths other
than those derived from the hierarchy of social values. In the
twenty-sixth story, on the other hand, where the values are
spiritual rather than social, the death of the virtuous lady the
young d'Avannes loves completes his spiritual education and thus
vindicates the higher truths by which she lived, truths not to be
found in Amadour's world. True, her death has none of the
cosmic overtones accompanying the disappearance of the *donna
angelicata*, but its profoundly sobering effect on the young lover is
indicated by the conclusion, which informs us of his return to
court, "où il demeura beaucoup d'années, sans vouloir ne veoir ne
parler à femme du monde, pour le regret qu'il avoit de sa dame; et
porta plus de dix ans le noir."[125] In Amadour's case, where
repression rather than sublimation of desire is called for, the
aggressive fantasy of the knight breaks through the veneer of
courtliness and destroys the pattern of idealized love which
permitted the amorous relationship with Floride; with d'Avannes,
the fantasy is brought under control by its counterpart, the fantasy
according to which the lover must suffer and sublimate his erotic
impulses. And his education is successful precisely because he is
allowed to test both patterns of amatory experience and is then
guided to a choice between the two.

The steps in this veritable education of a prince are interesting
to follow. At first, when he is fifteen, the young d'Avannes is not
really interested in women; he takes greater pleasure "à saulter et
dancer, que à regarder la beaulté des dames."[126] When he reaches
the age of seventeen, he falls in love with the virtuous wife of the
man in whose house he resides, but he is still so raw that he fears
this love and, "combien qu'il eust plus voluntiers aymé la saige
dame que nulle, ... la paour qu'il avoit de perdre son amityé...

[125] Novella 26, p. 219.     [126] *Ibid.*, p. 209.

le feit taire et se amuser ailleurs."[127] He therefore selects a
beautiful woman whose reputation for lightness makes her a more
accessible target and, having introduced himself into her household
in the guise of a groom, becomes her lover. This experience
provides him with full initiation into physical love, but the sexual
excesses of this first affair lay him low, and he returns to the house
of his friends in order to recover from their ill-effects. He is now
ready to begin his initiation into true spiritual maturity, and since
his first experience has apparently given him the confidence he
lacked before, he begins to woo his lady platonically, turning the
ladder of love on its head as he argues that his love of God has led
him to her:

> ...entendez que Dieu, incongneu de l'homme, sinon par la foy, a
> daigné prendre la chair semblable à celle de peché, afin qu'en
> attirant nostre chair à l'amour de son humanité, tirast aussi nostre
> esprit à l'amour de sa divinité; et s'est voulu servyr des moyens
> visibles, pour nous faire aymer par foy les choses invisibles. Aussy,
> ceste vertu que je desire aymer toute ma vie, est chose invisible,
> sinon par les effectz du dehors; parquoy, est besoing qu'elle prenne
> quelque corps pour se faire congnoistre entre les hommes, ce qu'elle
> a faict, se revestant du vostre pour le plus parfaict qu'elle a pu
> trouver; parquoy, je vous recongnois et confesse non seullement
> vertueuse, mais la seulle vertu; et, moy, qui la voys reluire soubz le
> vele du plus parfaict corps qui oncques fut, la veulx servir et
> honnorer toute ma vie, laissant pour elle toute autre amour vaine et
> vicieuse.[128]

Despite his noble declaration, it is still the lady's body he is drawn
to, and the kiss which he steals from her only inflames him
further so that he next tries to jump into bed with her. His
rashness earns him a severe reprimand, but he takes comfort from
the realization that his lady is not really angry with him but pities
him. Still he must live with his frustrated desires, and it is only
her deathbed confession of her love for him which opens his eyes to

[127] *Ibid.*, p. 210. The contrast between 'sage' and 'folle' is intended to echo the
parable of the wise and foolish virgins (*Matt.* 25: 1-13).
[128] *Ibid.*, pp. 214-215. This is essentially the argument, if not the spirit, to be
found later in Donne's *The Ecstasie*.

124

the true nobility of her character. Interestingly enough, the tenor of her speech is strongly reminiscent of Laura's declaration to Petrarch in the *Triumph of Death*, where she explains to the poet that she hid her love from him in order to safeguard her honor and lead him to virtue.[129] Marguerite's lady gives a similar account of her behavior as she declares that she kept her love secret in order to insure the safety of her conscience and her reputation; and although she does not claim that her purpose was to lead her lover to virtue, she nonetheless feels that she has accomplished this end, for she urges d'Avannes to continue addressing his love to virtuous ladies as she is sure that his grace, beauty, and moral character will make his love bear fruit.[130] Her exemplary death finally refines his sensibility and drives home to him the spirit of the theoretical Platonism he has so complacently spouted; he learns the true meaning of virtue and realizes the extent of his loss. As with the stilnovists, the death of the lady is necessary to effect a spiritual change in the lover, and the ten years' mourning is the external sign of the inner process of spiritual purification that is taking place.

These, then, are the stories in which Marguerite de Navarre covers the entire range of amatory relations between the sexes that can be readily placed on the various rungs of the *scala d'amore*. But, as I have already observed, the Neoplatonic ladder presents too narrow a structure within which to encompass human love, and offers too restricted a basis for a discussion which will take into account the instinctual nature of erotic drives as well as the spiritual aspirations of lovers. And since Marguerite's design is not so much to perpetuate the idealizing fantasies embodied in the aristocratic codes of love as to appraise actual human practice, she must necessarily seek a broader theoretical foundation for her discussion than that provided by traditional doctrine. The conversations which follow each of the stories give her the scope she needs, and offer her commentator his richest material.

129 *Triumphus Mortis*, 88-120, 139-159.
130 "... la grace, beaulté et honnesteté qui sont en vous ne permectent que vostre amour sans fruict travaille." Novella 26, p. 218.

# CHAPTER IV / WORLD OF MANY LOVES:
## THE DISCUSSIONS

At the root of Marguerite's investigation of love lies the assumption that love is in essence good and that it is the vagaries of human nature which can twist it to evil ends: in Saffredent's words, "tout ainsy que amour faict faire aux meschans des meschancetez, en ung cueur honneste faict faire choses dignes de louanges; car, amour, de soy, est bon, mais la malice du subgect luy faict souvent prendre ung nouveau surnom de fol, legier, cruel, ou villain."[1] So much is tacitly agreed upon by all the interlocutors, none of whom disputes Nomerfide's assertion that "la personne qui ayme parfaictement d'un amour joinct au commandement de son Dieu, ne congnoist honte ni deshonneur... car la gloire de bien aymer ne congnoist nulle honte."[2] Love is nowhere formally condemned, but on no other idea is there unanimity in the *Heptameron*, where each member of the group has his own notion of where honor stops and shame begins, and each has his own conception of what constitutes 'bien aymer.'

Marguerite's own views are voiced by Parlamente, whose point of departure is the Neoplatonic doctrine that love is the creative force which draws man to God – a position implicit in her definition of perfect lovers cited in Chapter II.[3] But her view is set against other very different evaluations, some of which are based on entirely different theories, some of which are the expression of deep-seated traditional prejudices, but all of which are colored by the personalities of the people who voice them. There is no judicious exposition of a theory in the manner of a Socratic dialogue but rather the living clash of ideas in the market place. The reader may be somewhat disoriented at first, but because the

[1] Novella 25, disc., p. 207.   [2] Novella 40, disc., p. 279.
[3] See above, pp. 60-61.

positions the various speakers advance are so many extensions of their respective characters, fairly consistent lines of argument emerge and it becomes an easy matter to grasp the spectrum of conflicting ideas. Besides, what the method loses in clarity of presentation, it gains in liveliness: Marguerite has taken the subject of countless abstract discussions and philosophical disquisitions and turned it into something that excites the minds and hearts of her conversationalists – as it should, since it is a subject which touches on the very fabric of life.

There are ten participants in the discussions of the *Heptameron*, five men and five women. The ladies range from the elderly Bible-reading Oisille to the young Nomerfide, 'la plus folle' as Parlamente calls her, whose youth makes her impatient with serious discussion. Between these two we find 'la saige Parlamente,' younger than Oisille and gayer in spirit, but equally imbued with a sense of the seriousness of life; Ennasuitte, a fierce feminist; and Longarine, a judicious widow who takes a skeptical view of men and their motives. The men are Geburon, older than his companions and more objectively detached in his opinions; Hircan, a great nobleman proud of his aristocratic prerogatives, sensual, bold, and intelligent; Simontault, a lesser version of Hircan, whose anti-feminism carries a note of petulancy prompted by sentimental self-indulgence; Saffredent, who bows to the new fashion in manners imported from Italy, yet whose assumption of courtly polish in no way alters his cynical view of women; and the gentle Dagoucin, inveterate champion of pure idealism, who, in Nomerfide's words, "est si saige, que, pour mourir ne diroit une follye."[4] The relationships linking these people are not altogether clear, for we are told only that Hircan is Parlamente's husband, and that Simontault and Dagoucin are both her suitors. Saffredent, we gather, is suitor to Longarine, and although it is mentioned that he is married, no wife is assigned to him. According to the identification of characters made by scholars,[5] he should be the husband

4 Novella 11, disc., p. 89.          5 See above, p. 32, n. 55.

of Nomerfide, and Ennasuitte and Simontault should be spouses as well, but there is nothing in the text to bear out these theories. However, as the identity of Marguerite's models has no bearing on the substance of the discussions, we need not concern ourselves with the question, and it will suffice to keep in mind that the three ranking interlocutors, Oisille, Parlamente, and Hircan, stand for Louise de Savoie, Marguerite, and Henri d'Albret, and that consequently theirs are significant positions in the ideological battle waged in the conversations of the *Heptameron*.

Generally speaking, the battle lines are drawn between the sexes, with Hircan, Simontault, and Saffredent the champions of the cause of masculine aggressiveness and the ladies the defenders of the honor of women, a situation that recalls the usual pattern of the *Querelle des femmes*. That an echo of the conflict over the relative merits of either sex does intrude into the conversations of the *Heptameron* is inevitable, for any book which deals with love has as its subject the virtues and failings of the sexes.[6] If the ladies extol chastity, the men decry hypocrisy or unnatural behavior, and if the men insist on the primacy of the natural drives, the ladies condemn lust and warn against dishonor – it is the age-old conflict between private passion and social restraint that animates their discussions. The aim, however, unlike that of the majority of literary treatises of love, is not the elaboration of an esthetically satisfying fantasy but the search for a resolution which will conciliate the contradictory dictates of desire, morality, and social decorum.

That love is a universal force operating within the context of a Christian universe is established not only by the interlocutors' habit of beginning each day with a reading from the Bible followed by attendance at mass, but also by repeated reference to the doctrine of grace. Marguerite places the thesis, developed at length in the third book of her *Prisons*, that man is nothing in the face of the absolute that is God, into the mouths of several of her

[6] On the *Querelle* in the *Heptameron* see Telle, *op. cit.*

conversationalists, who declare in one fashion or another that without God's help man is weak and prone to sin. Oisille, the champion of the private study of the Bible, is naturally the most consistent exponent of the doctrine, and as early as the second story she reminds her companions of their frailty by quoting a pronouncement she erroneously attributes to the Bible: "Ne nous resjouissons de nos vertuz, mais en ce que nous sommes escriptz au livre de Vie, duquel ne nous peult effacer Mort, Enfert ne Peché."[7] In a similar vein, commenting on a case of adultery, she expresses the wish to her friends that God might keep them all, for, as she says, "si sa bonté ne nous retient, il n'y a aucun d'entre nous qui ne puisse faire pis; mais ayant confiance en luy, il gardera celles qui confessent ne se pouvoir par elles-mesmes garder; et celles qui se confient en leurs forces sont en grand dangier d'estre tentées jusques à confesser leur infirmité."[8]

Saffredent also declares that "se fault recommander à Dieu, car, s'il ne nous tient à force, nous prenons grand plaisir à tresbucher,"[9] and Parlamente presents the maxim that "le premier pas que l'homme marche en la confiance de soy-mesmes, s'esloigne d'autant de la confiance de Dieu."[10] But Oisille goes even further when she insists that salvation can come only from God and rejects the idea of intermediaries between man and the deity. She echoes the spirit of the Reformation when she tells her listeners that she feels compelled to relate the twenty-third novella in order that

> l'ypocrisye de ceulx qui s'estiment plus religieux que les autres, ne vous enchante l'entendement, de sorte que vostre foy, divertye de son droict chemin, estime trouver salut en quelque autre creature que en Celluy qui n'a voulu avoir compaignon à nostre creation et redemption, lequel est tout puissant pour nous saulver en la vie eternelle, et, en ceste temporelle, nous consoler et delivrer de toutes noz tribulations.[11]

[7] Novella 2, disc., p. 21. The Apocalypse several times mentions the names of the elect inscribed in the Book of Life, but nowhere does the quotation appear as cited by Marguerite.
[8] Novella 32, disc., p. 245.
[9] Novella 30, disc., p. 234.
[10] Ibid., p. 233.
[11] Novella 22, disc., p. 186.

This warning appears in the context of sharp criticism leveled at the clergy in the wake of the tale of Sister Marie Héroet's tribulations, but the caution against seeking salvation in another person rather than in God may also apply to the infatuated romantic lover. Love and nature are compelling masters, but the power they wield over human beings is placed there by God, and even Hircan, their stanch advocate, agrees that it is best not to struggle single-handedly against their force but "se retirer au vray Amy et luy dire avecq le Psalmiste: 'Seigneur, je souffre force, respondez pour moy'."[12] There are no atheists, then, or religious skeptics among the speakers of the *Heptameron*, only sinners of greater or lesser degree who accept the fact of God's rule even when they disobey it. Hircan's succinct admission that "le peché me desplaist bien, et je suis marry d'offenser Dieu, mais le peché me plaist tousjours"[13] illustrates the dilemma of the man who chooses the law of his desires instead of the moral restraint demanded by God. And in the last analysis it is Geburon's conclusion that wishing for a more indulgent God will not bring him about, "parquoy fault obeyr à celluy que nous avons,"[14] which prevails. The Christian order, therefore, remains unchallenged.[15]

The divine order, then, is unquestionably the ultimate reality towards which all human beings should strive, but the reality Marguerite focuses on in the *Heptameron* is that of the sublunar world and its lovers. The relationship between the two worlds, considered at length in the *Prisons*,[16] is merely suggested, but never explored, in the discussions. The poem is therefore a helpful adjunct to the study of the *Heptameron*, for these two and the

---

[12] Novella 30, disc., p. 233. The quotation is actually from *Isaiah*, 38 : 14.
[13] Novella 25, disc., p. 207.
[14] *Ibid.*, p. 207.
[15] We should expect no less from a disciple of Lefèvre d'Etaples and Briçonnet. Besides, Febvre, in *Le Problème de l'incroyance au XVIe siècle*, has shown that this is generally true of sixteenth-century humanist thought in France.
[16] See above, p. 25, n. 30.

*Comédie de Mont-de-Marsan* are the product of the same ripened experience and mature feeling.

The form of autobiographical narrative which the *Prisons* assumes permits an explicit development of ideas to which the polemic dialogues of the other two do not lend themselves. It is especially useful in relation to Marguerite's appraisal of love, for in place of the contradictory positions espoused by the narrators of the *Heptameron*, we have the unified experience of one man who has run the gamut of the ladder of love from devoted courtly lover to lover of God. Marguerite's hero does not follow the facile rationalism of Castiglione's courtier by moving in smooth transition from the lady to the divine essence; his career is rather more akin to that of Dante, since his shattering disillusionment with idealistic love causes him to lose his way, to bend his energy to the pursuit of pleasure, ambition, and secular knowledge. It is the last of these that readies him for the final ascent to God. This ascent is no longer undertaken under the guidance of a *donna angelicata* but with the inspiration derived from the Bible – one more indication of Marguerite's evangelism, which far from rejecting the world, accepts it for what it is and seeks to trace the path that will lead through it to God.

This refusal to turn her back on the world of the living may explain Marguerite's qualms about courtly love, especially when it is at its purest. Despite the idealism which informs it, she recognizes its essentially narcissistic character: the total identification of the lover with his lady only leads him back to himself and keeps him imprisoned in a passion which "se peult dire y dolatre" (*Prisons*, p. 165). This love is natural to man, however, and Amateur, the old man who is instrumental in effecting the hero's salvation by introducing him to wisdom and the Bible, is an orthodox Renaissance Neoplatonist when he explains to his friend that his heart was drawn to desire the beauty sensed by his eyes.[17] Not only is this love

[17] "Vos jeunes yeulx ont vostre cueur tiré     A quoy bien fort l'a poulsé la nature
A la beaulté, puys il a desiré               Que Dieu a myse en toute creature:
De ce bien là, dont avoit congnoissance,     C'est un vouloir de se perpetuer."
Par ung plaisir en avoir jouyssance,                         (*Prisons*, p. 164)

natural, prompted by the Dionian Venus,[18] but it is virtuous since it contents itself with the pleasures of speech and sight,[19] and it is this restraint which defines *fin amor:*

> Aussi le vray amour a tel povoir
> Que qui le peult parfaictement avoir
> Et en remplir son cueur entierement,
> De nul desir ny craincte n'a tourment;
> Qui a desir de myeulx et de pis craincte
> N'a jamais eu d'amour la vive attaincte....[20]

Here this voluntary restraint leads to a state of emotional stasis rather than to the inner perturbations traditionally associated with passion, a movement which is also in keeping with the rationalist bias of Neoplatonic psychology: once the so-called lower instincts are brought under the control of reason, peace and harmony reign in the soul, whose progress is then guided by the intellect. But neither the prisoner of the poem nor Dagoucin, the exponent of this type of ideality in the *Heptameron*, takes the subsequent step on the Neoplatonic ladder of love, and their passion becomes an end in itself instead of leading to a higher degree of spiritual awareness. For Marguerite, the conclusion that courtly love imprisons rather than liberates is inevitable; such love must therefore ultimately be rejected, the prison ultimately broken.

The self-centered isolation from the world, and therefore from life, induced by the idealized love fantasy is aptly described by the hero of the *Prisons* when he tells his lady that

> J'estoys donq roy, car j'aymoys si très fort
> Qu'il n'y avoit fin en moy que la mort;
> Et vous tenoys par amour aprouvée
> Semblable à moy, vous ayant esprouvée.[21]

---

[18] See above, Chapter II, p. 44.
[19] "... le parler et le regard des yeulx / ... De soy, sans plus, vostre cueur contanta" (*Prisons*, pp. 164-165).
[20] *Ibid.*, p. 165.       [21] *Ibid.* p. 127.

If not for the lady's inconstancy, he would have remained forever in the prison of love fashioned by his own desire; as Amateur subsequently explains to him,

> ... sans avoir du soleil la lumiere
> Qui vous monstra muable et mensongere
> Celle que tant teniez loyalle et ferme,
> Jamais n'eussiez sailly hors de ce terme.[22]

From a superficial point of view the state the prisoner was in may be morally preferable to the active pursuit of sexual gratification he engages in afterwards, but neither way of life is satisfactory since both shut him off from God. For that matter the latter state may actually be the better, despite surface appearances to the contrary, in the same way that La Mondaine's dedication to worldly concerns is deemed superior to La Superstitieuse's narrow-mindedness in the *Comédie de Mont-de-Marsan:* just as the worldly lady's conduct is at least an affirmation of the physical foundations of life (an affirmation her superstitious sister does not make for *her* lack of generosity rejects God's gift of life and makes a mockery of divine love) so the prisoner's active participation in the life of the world is better than his self-willed incarceration in an illusory paradise of love. Reality, which first intrudes upon him in the guise of his lady's mutability, is painful because it shatters his cozy dream world and exposes the vanity of human ambition, but the disillusionment paves the way for the revelation of the divine order he encounters in God's resounding "I am that I am" in the Bible, a declaration which unlocks the secret of existence for him and leads him to salvation.[23] The Bible can be a guide through the maze of life to the supreme truth that is God only after man has subjected himself to the test of living and has garnered the bitter fruits of experience; otherwise his is a sterile existence.

[22] *Ibid.*, p. 165.
[23] *Ibid.*, pp. 212-213: "Je suys qui suys fin et commencement...."

The notion that the courtly relationship of pure love ultimately points to death is also present in the *Heptameron*. When the question of the goals of love arises, Dagoucin champions the view that love's sole aim should be to love perfectly, but his understanding of perfection differs markedly from that of Parlamente, with whom he is generally in agreement. Where, according to her, perfect lovers are those who seek in one another some ideal, the search for which eventually brings them to God, Dagoucin says that the passion aroused in the lover should content him so thoroughly that he need seek no further gratification. Parlamente at least bases her definition on the premise of a relationship between the lover and his lady, but her arch-idealistic friend refuses to admit such a relationship because he wishes to protect the idealization of love from the imperfections of human nature which might otherwise destroy his fantasy. He asserts that

> si nostre amour est fondée sur la beaulté, bonne grace, amour et faveur d'une femme, et nostre fin soit plaisir, honneur ou proffict, l'amour ne peult longuement durer; car, si la chose sur quoy nous la fondons default, nostre amour s'envolle hors de nous. Mais je suis ferme à mon oppinion, que celluy qui ayme, n'ayant autre fin ne desir que bien aymer, laissera plus tost son ame par la mort, que ceste forte amour saille de son cueur.[24]

He neatly circumvents the unfortunate experience of the lady's mutability which opened the prisoner's eyes in *Les Prisons* by divorcing passion from its object. To him, the only end of love is to love well. When Simontault challenges him, declaring that he can never have been in love, and accusing him of depicting "la chose publicque de Platon, qui s'escript et ne s'experimente poinct,"[25] Dagoucin explains further:

> Si j'ay aymé, ... j'ayme encores, et aymeray tant que je vivray. Mais j'ay si grand paour que la demonstration face tort à la perfection de mon amour, que je crainctz que celle de qui je debvrois desirer

[24] Novella 8, disc., p. 48.          [25] *Ibid.*, p. 48.

l'amityé semblable, l'entende; et mesmes je n'ose penser ma pensée, de paour que mes oeilz en revelent quelque chose; car, tant plus je tiens ce feu celé et couvert, et plus en joy croist le plaisir de sçavoir que j'ayme parfaictement.[26]

Dagoucin has extended the call for secrecy in love to include the lady, for only by confining his passion to the secret recesses of his heart and mind can the lover be sure of safeguarding the inviolability of both his ideal and his feelings. Although he readily admits that to be loved would be deeply gratifying, he refuses to make it the goal of desire. He insists on sundering the complementary facets – loving and being loved – of the amatory relationship in order to preserve the ideal of true love in its uncompromising subjectivity: "Quant je seroys tant aymé que j'ayme," he declares, "si n'en sçauroit croistre mon amour, comme elle ne sçauroit diminuer pour n'estre si très aymé que j'ayme fort."[27] Such high-mindedness may have appealed to the idealistic Marguerite who had come under the influence of Pocque and Quintin,[28] but she recognized the life-denying quality of a fantasy which divests emotion of its tangible goals and immures the lover in the cloistered contemplation of his feelings. The point, made only once in the *Heptameron*, is never again picked up in the discussions, but its import is unmistakable. Parlamente, we are told, "soupsonnoit ceste fantaisye,"[29] and she consequently exclaims, "Donnez-vous garde, Dagoucin; car j'en ay veu d'aultres que vous, qui ont mieulx aymé mourir que parler."[30] Her friend's reply that he deems such people extremely happy only lends weight to the suspicion that his ideal of true love tends to seek fulfillment in death. Unlike his masculine companions who find him terribly foolish, he fervently holds to the conviction that the death resulting from perfect love is the highest proof of the quality of one's passion, and as such is glorious. We may be sure that he would endorse wholeheartedly Petrarch's well known "Che bel fin fa chi ben amando more."[31]

[26] *Ibid.*, p. 48.  [28] See above, Chapter I, pp. 24 ff.  [30] *Ibid.*, p. 48.
[27] *Ibid.*, p. 48.  [29] Novella 8, disc., p. 48.  [31] *In Vita*, CXL.

Though courtly idealism does not inevitably lead to Christian Revelation, and may even, as in the case of Marguerite's prisoner, effectively isolate the lover from it, the two are nonetheless related in the Queen's mind, for she was too much of a Neo-platonist not to feel that all forms of love must ultimately stem from the principle of divine love which brought the world into being. As several passages in the *Prisons* indicate, she had in her later years adopted the Neoplatonic definition of the final goal of love as her own, for it was consistent with the fundamental Christian faith which saw in the Incarnation God's second great gift of love to mankind. In the *Miroir de l'âme pécheresse* she had succumbed to a mood of self-denigration, seeing herself mired in the pollution of the flesh from which only a rather cheerless divine grace could rescue her, but in the later poem Neoplatonism helps her resolve triumphantly the depressing Calvinist dichotomy as she perceives in man's humanity the divine spark which enables him to transcend the confines of the flesh and join himself to God in a true spiritual union only love makes possible. Love, as the hero proclaims, is

> ... le vray moyen
> Que l'homme est homme et sans lequel n'est rien:
> Celluy qui Est en cest amour je voy,
> Il est qui Est, et a son estre en soy,
> Bien qu'il soit filz du grant Dieu d'habundance,
> Ayant pris chair subjecte à indigence;
> Son povoir vient de la divinité
> Et son tourment de nostre humanité,
> Dont sort Amour, ce divin feu brullant,
> Qui va tout autre amour anihilant.[32]

The somber mood of Marguerite's middle years has been transmuted into a glorious vision of human redemption. But while the older, wiser Marguerite of the *Prisons* and the *Heptameron* takes the Christian Platonists' conception of love for granted, she does not view the process of love in exactly the same light as theirs. From the point of view of doctrine the difference is perhaps no more than a

[32] *Prisons*, pp. 216-217.

change in emphasis, Marguerite lending greater weight to the Dionian principle, but the change is the logical consequence of a markedly different evaluation of human nature. Where Neoplatonism underlines the spiritual nature of man, a rational being who, guided by his intellect, may proceed in orderly fashion along the ascending *scala d'amore*, the Queen of Navarre keeps her gaze fixed firmly on his animal nature and perceives that his appetitive will, reinforced by his original fall from grace, presents a more formidable obstacle to spiritual growth than the Neoplatonists recognize. Her concern, after all, is not with the elaboration of a metaphysical system but with its application to everyday life, a concern which causes her to keep close contact with psychological reality. Hers is the more dramatic vision, even in the *Prisons*, for she sees man's spiritual progress as a struggle in which he tests, through trial and error, the various avenues to the fulfillment of desire the world opens to him; it is only when these have been exhausted without bringing him the peace he craves that he is ready for that leap into the Beyond which will reveal the Love that annihilates all other loves. In short, it is man's experience of life, far more than the independent operation of his intellect, which brings him to the point where he can comprehend the divine message contained in the Bible, and even then the final illumination comes, not as the product of rational deduction, but as a sudden shock of recognition under grace which shakes the very foundations of his being.

Love, then, is to be tested by experience before it can effectively lead the lover to God. Dagoucin's ideal is not acceptable to Marguerite, for his concept of passion is completely self-contained, precluding contact with *any* objective reality, be it God or the world. None of the stories even illustrates this doctrine since it does not allow for an objective situation around which to build a plot; even Dagoucin's story designed to convince his audience that one can die for loving too well requires the frustration of unrequited love to bring about the lover's demise.[33] In spite of her

33 Novella 9. See above, Chapter III, pp. 74-77.

very real interest in Neoplatonism, Marguerite never capitalizes on Dagoucin's avowed detachment from human entanglement to take him further along the ladder of love and provide her readers with an illustration of philosophic love. That she does not confirms our conviction of her interest in the relationship between the sexes rather than in the philosophical definition of love. Even Parlamente's Platonist declaration of faith is presented in the guise of a definition of perfect *lovers*, and the reciprocal nature of love is always affirmed: the lovers may ultimately be joined in God, but the relationship linking them together is never completely relinquished.[34]

In the world of human desire, the stage for the *Heptameron's* stories, the central fact about man's amatory experience is his sensual nature with its overriding drive to satisfaction. Love begins as physical attraction – it has to, since the desire for physical union is naturally implanted in man to insure the perpetuation of the race. This view places love in the realm of the instincts and, in the *Heptameron*, provides the basis for Hircan's powerful advocacy of the naturalness of physical drives and their fulfillment. Parlamente's husband is not a Neoplatonist: unlike his friends Saffredent and Simontault, he is far from having absorbed either the doctrine or the manners that have come from Italy, and he remains essentially the *grand seigneur*, proud of his prowess as warrior and lover, for whom love is only an adventure designed to satisfy his desires. He has no use for the fearful, passive lover; true love is so powerful an inducement to action that

---

[34] Novella 19, the story of Poline and her lover (see above, Chapter III, pp. 70-71), is a case in point. The lovers, thwarted by the worldliness of their masters, retire from the world, but even the monastic life fails to destroy the spiritual bond between them: "Ce serviteur religieux... luy fortiffia son oppinion le plus qu'il luy fut possible, luy disant que, puis qu'il ne povoit plus avoir d'elle au monde autre chose que la parolle, il se tenoit bien heureux d'estre en lieu où il auroit toujours moyen de la recouvrer, et qu'elle seroit telle, que l'un et l'aultre n'en pourroit que mieulx valloir, vivans en ung estat d'un amour, d'un cueur et d'un esperit tirez et conduictz de la bonté de Dieu, lequel il supplioit les tenir en sa main, en laquelle nul ne peut perir." Novella 19, p. 150.

nothing will make the lover stop short of success. He declares that "je ne me departiray de la forte opinion que j'ay, que oncques homme qui aymast parfaictement, ou qui fust aymé d'une dame, ne failloit d'en avoir bonne yssue, s'il a faict la poursuicte comme il appartient."[35] His motto is that 'faint heart never won fair lady': the lover must use force, if necessary, to overcome the socially induced resistance of women. For, he argues, Nature has endowed women with the very same desires it has bestowed upon men. Only false pride and social convention cause them to refuse the demands of their suitors:

> ... car, si leur honneur n'en estoit non plus taché que le nostre, vous trouveriez, que Nature n'a rien oblyé en elles non plus que en nous; et, pour la contraincte que elles se font de n'oser prendre le plaisir qu'elles desirent, ont changé ce vice en ung plus grand qu'elles tiennent plus honneste. C'est une gloire et cruaulté, par qui elles esperent acquerir nom d'immortalité, et ainsy se gloriffi-ans de resister au vice de la loy de Nature (si Nature est vicieuse), se font non seullement semblables aux bestes inhumaines et cruelles, mais aux diables, desquelz elles prennent l'orgueil et la malice.[36]

It is by virtue of this 'loy de Nature' that Hircan justifies his as-sertion that the true end of love is not adoration, but possession of the lady. To deny this aim is unnatural and may lead to tragic consequences, and he adduces the incest of the thirtieth tale as a warning to "celles qui cuydent par leurs forces et vertu vaincre amour et nature avecq toutes les puissances que Dieu y a mises."[37] While the notion of 'natural law' operating at the root of human desire is not inconsistent with Neoplatonic or Christian doctrine, Hircan's line of reasoning is. He thus finds himself in complete opposition to Dagoucin, whose view of human nature he cannot accept. When Dagoucin argues that the perfect lover is one who cherishes his lady's honor above all else and seeks only "une response honneste et gratieuse, telle que parfaicte et honneste

---

[35] Novella 10, disc., p. 83.        [37] Novella 30, disc., p. 233.
[36] Novella 26, disc., p.220.

amityé requiert,"[38] and insists on secrecy in one's love not only as a measure of the depth of passion[39] but also as a safeguard against the slander of those who cannot conceive of a virtuous attachment,[40] Hircan replies that he is being unrealistic: "Je vous asseure, Dagoucin, ... que vous avez une si haulte philosophie, qu'il n'y a homme icy qui l'entende ne la croye; car vous nous vouldriez faire acroyre que les hommes sont anges, ou pierres, ou diables."[41] Dagoucin objects that some there are who would rather die than have a lady violate her conscience for their pleasure; Hircan declares that every man seeks possession in love and that anyone who disclaims such desire is just crying 'sour grapes.'[42] Similarly, when Dagoucin, rejecting Simontault's call for freedom to follow openly one's bent in affairs of the heart, declares that "ceulx qui aymeroient mieulx mourir, que leur volonté fust congneue, ne se pourroient accorder à vostre ordonnance,"[43] Hircan reiterates his deep-seated disbelief in the existence of such lovers: "Mourir!... encor est-il à naistre le bon chevalier qui pour telle chose publicque vouldroit mourir."[44] In short, the fulfillment of love is to be found only in physical consummation, and the lover who cannot attain it with one lady had better seek gratification elsewhere – as far as he is concerned, says Hircan, "l'on ne me sçauroit faire si peu de mauvaise chere, que incontinant je ne laisse l'amour et la dame ensemble."[45]

Such a position is that of the aggressive male who insists on the primacy of his erotic drive. The masculine code of honor Hircan espouses requires the lover to banish all fear, to use force if necessary to achieve his end; it applies to love the principles of

[38] Novella 12, disc., p. 95.
[39] "on dit que l'amour la plus secrete est la plus louable." Novella 42, disc., p. 295.
[40] "... fault aussy bien cacher quant l'amour est vertueuse, que si elle estoit au contraire, pour ne tomber au mauvais jugement de ceulx qui ne peuvent croire que ung homme puisse aymer une dame par honneur." Novella 53, disc., p. 341.
[41] Ibid., p. 341.    [42] "...ilz font semblant de n'aymer poinct les raisins quand ilz sont si haults, qu'ilz ne les peuvent cueillir." Ibid., p. 341.
[43] Novella 14, disc., p. 115.    [44] Ibid., p. 115.    [45] Novella 15, disc., p. 128.

140

war. Hircan criticizes lovers who back down in the face of feminine resistance: Amadour, he says, would not have failed in his attack on Floride if he had been more of a lover and less of a coward,[46] and as for the would-be rapist of the fourth tale, "son cueur n'estoit pas tout plain d'amour, veu que la craincte de mort et de honte y trouva encores place."[47] He has no use for the masochistic passitivy of the idealistic lover, and, he tells the assembled group, had *he* been the one trying to take the princess of Flanders by force, he would have felt dishonored at not having brought an attempted forcible conquest to a successful conclusion; he would therefore have killed the old lady-in-waiting who was helping her mistress defend herself and taken the princess.[48] In other words, the sexual prerogative of the male, his by virtue of his greater strength, is not to be denied.[49]

If Hircan were merely the exponent of a rather primitive and facile sensualism, he would not deserve to be taken very seriously – the sensuality of human beings is a fact that both Neoplatonism and orthodox Christianity readily take in stride. But his view of love extends beyond the limited conception of the professional amorist who, like Saffredent, tends to see in it no more than an elaborate game of courtship having as its aim the conquest of the lady. Invoking the rule of Nature, he implicitly formulates a doctrine which is to serve as a rationale for human behavior and becomes no less a moralist than his chief opponent in debate, Parlamente. He, too, accepts original sin and, like the idealists, conceives of love as a universal force; but where they would found its action in the soul's desire for salvation, he sees it as a powerful agent of man's instinctual life and reminds his audience that it has been rooted in Nature by none other than God Himself.[50]

[46] His words are "plus amoureux que crainctif." Novella 10, disc., p. 83.
[47] Novella 4, disc., p. 34.
[48] *Ibid.*, p. 34.
[49] The point is illustrated in several tales; see above, Chapter III, pp. 86-87, 89-91.
[50] See above, p. 139.

What is ultimately at issue between Hircan and the idealists is whether the so-called higher or lower faculties direct the life of man. To Hircan the evidence of the senses is incontrovertible — the body through which he knows himself, the desires he feels, are far more tangibly real than the soul and its heavenly aspirations. To deny the appetitive basis of desire seems to him an exercise in nonsense or, worse, hypocrisy, and to refuse the body its due in love is the height of folly since it frustrates a desire inherently natural and transforms what should be a happy experience into something painful. Considering Poline and her lover mad, he refuses to join in their praise: "Si melencolie et desespoir sont louables, je diray que Poline et son serviteur sont bien dignes d'être louez."[51] The primary psychic order in man is derived from below (the body) and not from above (the soul) as the idealists would have it, and any attempt to invert this order distorts nature.

Hircan is by no means a facile sensualist; he merely insists that sexual gratification is an integral part of the love experience. For that matter, his sensualism is disciplined. The story he relates of the gentleman student who willingly controls his libidinous impulses under very trying circumstances to secure his lady's love and establish an emotionally rewarding relationship with her is told in praise of the lover.[52] But all lovers worthy of the name desire nothing less than physical completeness. As human nature is one and the same regardless of sex, he rejects Parlamente's attempt to distinguish between the love of women, which, she says, is founded in God and honor and is therefore just and reasonable, and that of men, founded in pleasure: however much faces and clothes may differ in men and women, the will is the same.[53] Nor is this will particularly virtuous; man's nature inclines him to sin, and Hircan is even something of a Calvinist (however unwittingly) when he declares that "la nature des femmes et des hommes est de soy

[51] Novella 19, disc., p. 151; see above, Chapter III, pp. 70 ff.
[52] Novella 18; see above, Chapter III, pp. 115-117.
[53] "... si croy-je que les voluntez sont toutes pareilles." Novella 21, disc., p. 175.

incline à tout vice, si elle n'est preservée de Celluy à qui l'honneur de toute victoire doibt estre rendu."[54] Worldly-proud aristocrat that he is, though, Hircan uses such denigration of human nature not as a call to reform but as proof of the rightness of his call to sexuality. Man's libidinous drives may, in some ultimate sense, be sinful; but, he seems to be saying, that's how man is, and nothing anyone says can change him.

At heart Hircan is a materialist for whom the ideal world is one in which God's will would be in harmony with man's desires.[55] But since such a world apparently is not possible, he is content to enjoy the pleasures attendant upon his state while leaving the rest to God – his business is with this world and not with the next. He differs radically from Parlamente and Oisille, both of whom refuse to see in the fall of man an excuse for burying the divine spark that animates him. Where Hircan sees life as a naturally enjoyable process – much in the spirit of Leo X's "Since God gave us the Papacy, now let's enjoy it!" – they perceive potentially tragic overtones in man's separation from God, and find the meaning of life in his endeavor to make his way back to the heaven he lost. Oisille, because of her age, is somewhat detached in her judgment of human beings; she has made her peace with the world, and more and more she turns to the Bible for consolation and inspiration. Parlamente, on the other hand, is still in the mainstream of life; it is she, therefore, who bears the brunt of the battle in opposition to her husband's doctrine.

We have seen that, although she may sympathize with the nobility of Dagoucin's ideal, Parlamente rejects it as sterile. What, then, does she propose as an alternative to Hircan's materialism? Her program is contained in her impassioned definition of perfect lovers: two people who, in their attachment for one another, seek an ideal above the materialism of life, an ideal which ultimately is God. Love is not, as Hircan would have it, merely an emanation

[54] Novella 34, disc., p. 254.
[55] Cf. the passage in which he expresses the wish that his pleasure would please God as much as it pleases him, Novella 25, disc., p. 207.

of the senses, but a truly spiritual phenomenon, the source of which is to be found in the Creator. While Parlamente never denies the reality of the flesh and of what Hircan calls Nature, she knows that man is possessed of an immortal soul. Therefore, a proper evaluation of the human situation requires a recognition of that soul's desire to seek its Maker. She agrees that man is sinful by nature and needs God's help to overcome his weaknesses, but she believes that the soul, divine in origin, participates actively in the process of salvation during its pilgrimage on earth. Love makes this participation possible; however, as man is deeply mired in the flesh, love manifests itself first as desire for earthly objects, and only gradually can man reach the understanding that his desire is nothing other than his soul's yearning to return to its heavenly home. In short, she opposes to Hircan's spiritually restrictive notion of sexual drives the Neoplatonic vision of a transcendent force which links man to God – again, the only synthesizing answer available to Marguerite.

As I have already remarked, Parlamente's declaration of faith defines an ideal far more than it describes an actuality.[56] Her highly condensed presentation of the ladder of love, conveying, as it does, the essential rationale and spirit of the Neoplatonic ascent, suffers from the one defect characteristic of all such presentations: it fails to come to grips with the dynamics of a genuine interrelationship between two lovers. This omission is a necessary consequence of the Neoplatonic conception which sees in the beloved little more than an object of adoration that is merely the external occasion for the inner spiritual progress of the lover; once the lover has climbed beyond the first few rungs of the ladder, he loses sight of the beloved for she has no further function to perform in his life. Reciprocity of feeling is thus notoriously absent as a goal from the Neoplatonic love experience, a state of affairs rarely to be met with in life. We should therefore hardly expect the worldly-wise Queen of Navarre to advocate the

[56] See above, Chapter II, p. 61.

Neoplatonic design as a blueprint for the vast majority of man-kind; such a course would be both unrealistic and highly im-practical. If, however, we think of Neoplatonism as a philosophic movement which seeks to define the ideal – and therefore, in the Platonic sense, true – pattern which underlies the realities of the sensually perceived world, we can see that Parlamente's declaration opens rather than closes her part of the debate on love. Just as Castiglione fashioned the portrait of the *ideal* courtier to serve as a goal for courtiers, so Marguerite depicts the perfect lovers as an illustration of the ideal which will help define a line of conduct for real lovers. In this sense Neoplatonism becomes the point of departure for Parlamente's discussion of love; it is the *terminus a quo* for her argument, not the *terminus ad quem*.

On the other hand, when Parlamente defines a pattern for the conduct of real lovers, she sets high but not unreasonable stan-dards. Her problem is to conciliate the demands of passion with Christian doctrine and social decorum. She would like to see a love that is free from sin yet sufficiently real to provide the lovers with the emotional solace which is their right. She is sensible to the dangers of love, finding most dangerous the spiritual passion of the idealist tradition because its snares are less obvious than those of other forms of love;[57] but, unlike Longarine, who suggests it might be best to shun love altogether,[58] she is convinced of the

[57] "... l'exemple ... alleguée servira à celles qui cuydent que l'amour spirituelle ne soit poinct dangereuse. Mais il me semble qu'elle l'est plus que toutes les aultres ... [car] ... il n'est rien plus sot, ne plus aysé à tromper, que une femme qui n'a jamais aymé. Car amour de soy est une passion qui a plus tost saisy le cueur que l'on ne s'en advise; et est ceste passion si plaisante, que, si elle se peut ayder de la vertu, pour luy servir de manteau, à grand peyne sera-elle congneue, qu'il n'en vienne quelque inconvenient." Novella 35, disc., p. 260. The statement that spiritual love is more dangerous than all other forms may not be Parlamente's, for the editor precedes it with a dash (which usually indicates a new speaker) although he gives no name for that possible interlocutor. The remainder of the passage quoted here, appearing as a reply to a subsequent interruption, is explicitly attributed to Parlamente. The context, however, strongly suggests that even the passage in doubt is Parlamente's.
[58] Novella 70, disc., p. 418.

necessity of love in life. She believes firmly that no one can love God without first loving another human being, yet, worthy sister of Marguerite's La Sage, she mistrusts passion because it can so easily lead man astray. Unlike the wise lady of the play, Parlamente is endowed with practical common sense and a sense of humor, but hers is a serious view of love which rejects both the narcissism of Dagoucin's idealism and the callousness of Hircan's materialism. Her program for practical living calls for neither the soaring flight of Platonic idealism nor the reduction of feeling to its physical roots; she would anchor human conduct in obedience to God, respect for one's self, and attention to the amenities of social living.

The passion-induced excesses set forth in the tales would be sufficient to make Parlamente doubtful of the value of romantic love, but the praise bestowed on it by some of her companions makes her all the more aware of the necessity for controlling so disturbing a force. For she needs to deal not only with Hircan and Dagoucin, but also with the far more common view of love which, combining idealism with masculine aggressiveness, stands mid-way between the two extremes: the troubadours' theory of mixed love. Its chief exponents are Simontault and Saffredent, although all the interlocutors of the *Heptameron* share its position to greater or lesser degrees.

Simontault is the romantic who dreams of an ideal woman, for the love of whom the world might well be lost: "Voylà qui me plaist bien," he announces after hearing Longarine's tale of tragedy wrought by excessive love, "quant l'amour est si egalle, que, luy morant, l'autre ne vouloit plus vivre. Et si Dieu m'eust faict la grace d'en trouver une telle, je croy que jamais n'eust aymé plus parfaictement."[59] One suspects that the *Liebestod* motif of the story appeals to him, especially since the death of the lovers is intimately connected with the sexual act, but it is the longing for the lady's reward which ennobles man and gives meaning to the ideal of chivalry; for, still according to Simontault, "s'il estoit . . .

[59] Novella 50, disc., p. 325. On the story, see above, Chapter III, pp. 111-113.

que les dames fussent sans mercy, nous pourrions bien faire reposer nos chevaulx et faire rouller noz harnoys jusques à la premiere guerre, et ne faire que penser du mesnaige"[60] – a sentiment echoed by Dagoucin's declaration that "si nous pensions les dames sans amour, nous vouldrions estre sans vie. J'entends de ceux qui ne vivent que pour l'acquerir; et, encores qu'ilz n'y adviennent, l'esperance les soustient et leur faict faire mille choses honnorables.... Mais qui penseroit que les dames n'aymassent poinct, il fauldroit en lieu d'hommes d'armes, faire des marchans; et, en lieu d'acquerir honneur, ne penser que à amasser du bien."[61] Obviously, the troubadour doctrine linking love to the prowess of the professional knight was still popular in the sixteenth century if so pure an idealist as Dagoucin can voice it as a matter of course.

Marguerite's chief objection to Simontault's dream of an all-embracing passion, however, is that it is potentially destructive, for, whether it be 'pure' or 'mixed,' it deflects the soul from its proper goals. Oisille makes the point when she draws the moral of the *châtelaine* de Vergi's story: St. Paul, she says, would not allow this great passion even to married people because "d'autant que nostre cueur est affectionné à quelque chose terrienne, d'autant s'esloigne-il de l'affection celeste; et plus l'amour est honneste et vertueuse et plus difficille en est à rompre le lien."[62] Oisille, suggesting that this kind of passion is more properly addressed to God than to human beings, urges her friends "de demander à Dieu son Sainct Esperit, par lequel vostre amour soyt tant enflambée en l'amour de Dieu, que vous n'aiez poinct de peyne, à la mort, de laisser ce que vous aymez trop en ce monde."[63]

But Parlamente is skeptical of such idealism for other reasons, too. She replies to Simontault's outburst with the teasing suggestion that love would never cause *him* to neglect self-preservation, for the time is past when men forgot their lives for their ladies'

---

[60] Novella 56, disc., p. 352.
[61] Novella 70, disc., p. 419.

[62] *Ibid.*, p. 418.
[63] *Ibid.*, p. 418.

sakes.[64] Romantic idealism, she is saying in effect, is more often than not a 'line' men use to seduce women to their desires, and foolish is the woman who is taken in by it. The courtly suitor may propose an idealistic romance, but his intention usually lies in the direction of amorous dalliance. Her prejudice is justified by Hircan's brutal admission that he has never loved a woman, with the exception of his wife, "à qui il ne desirast faire offenser Dieu bien lourdement,"[65] and Saffredent's boast that the terms of courtly love are merely a device whereby the lover gets a hearing. For who is the woman, he asks, who will turn a deaf ear when a man begins talking of honor and virtue? But, he continues, "nous couvrons nostre diable du plus bel ange que nous pouvons trouver. Et, soubz ceste couverture, avant que d'estre congneuz, recepvons beaucoup de bonnes cheres. Et peut-estre tirons les cueurs des dames si avant que, pensans aller droict à la vertu, quand elles congnoissent le vice, elles n'ont le moyen ne le loisir de retirer leurs pieds."[66]

Though Saffredent may seem to be the cynic in this passage, he is merely voicing the evident truth that among civilized people love does not usually present itself in the form of unabashed sexual desire. Yet the poetry of romance nonetheless contains – masks, some would say – the very real presence of man's libidinous drives. Saffredent goes further, however, and steals the Neoplatonists' thunder by suggesting that 'mixed' love may not be so very sinful after all since it is the first step on the ladder which leads to love of God. Love is a 'furieuse follye' – obviously an echo of Ficino's 'furor' – not amenable to reason, no more than a venial sin which is easily forgiven. Furthermore, "Dieu ne se courrouce poinct de tel peché, veu que c'est ung degré pour monter à l'amour parfaicte de luy, où jamais nul ne monta, qu'il n'ait passé par

---

[64] Novella 50, disc., p. 325. Parlamente is contrasting him with the hero of the tale, who bled to death because, in the heat of passion, the bandage covering his wound came undone. See above, Chapter III, pp. 111-113.

[65] Novella 12, disc., p. 96.

[66] *Ibid.*, p. 96.

l'eschelle de l'amour de ce monde" – Parlamente's very doctrine.[67] And he concludes his defense of courtly love with a paraphrase of St. John: "Comment aymerez-vous Dieu, que vous ne voyez poinct, si vous n'aymez celluy que vous voyez?"[68]

Saffredent's apology may be no more than a cleverly impudent piece of sophistry – at least, so Oisille chooses to see it, as she cautions him against his all too facile borrowing from Holy Writ, but his argument deserves serious consideration. It voices a formidable defense of romantic passion, the strength and appeal of which reside in the fact that it accommodates the views of an Hircan, who would see in love the workings of 'Nature,' i.e., biological drives, with those of a Parlamente or Oisille, who would insist on the divine origin and import of love. Saffredent may be accused of confusing the spiritual and physical 'furores' of Ficino and combining them into his single 'furieuse follye,' but it is doubtful that the average literate courtier of his day kept the distinction in his mind and, what is more to the point, in his feelings. The conduct of love affairs remains unchanged; only the theory has been brought up to date with the inclusion of elements borrowed from Christian Neoplatonism. It is perhaps ironic that Saffredent should appropriate Parlamente's basic tenet that the path to God runs through the loves of this world, but his cleverness, together with his reference to the ladder of love, serves to buttress 'mixed' love against the attacks of orthodox Christianity and assuages in some measure the guilt attendant upon such affairs. Saffredent thus provides a rationale far more convincing than any to be found in Andreas.

Not only does the theory of 'mixed' love Saffredent develops dispose rather neatly of the problem of sin, but it also sets forth

[67] Novella 36, disc., p. 265. Cf. Parlamente's declaration that man will never love God perfectly unless he first loves someone perfectly in this world (cited above, Chapter II, p. 60).

[68] *Ibid.*, p. 265. The quotation is based on *i John* 4:20: "If a man say, I love God, and hateth his brother, he is a liar: for he that loveth not his brother whom he hath seen, how can he love God whom he hath not seen?"

the lover's dual pattern of behavior in relation to his mistress. Inherent in the passive-aggressive polarity of the fantasy which underlies the theory, the double line of conduct requires the lover to assume respectful obedience towards his lady in public, but demands that in private he exercise the rights of masterful conquest which his masculine superiority and, hopefully, the lady's gift of herself bestow upon him. The clash between the two is illustrated by Oisille's outcry against Hircan's suggestion that it was Amadour's duty to use force, if necessary, to gain possession of Floride. "Quel debvoir?" she asks him indignantly. "Appellez-vous faire son debvoir à ung serviteur qui veult avoir par force sa maistresse, à laquelle il doibt toute reverence et obeissance?"[69] Saffredent resolves the issue by drawing again the distinction between the public and private encounters of lovers:

> Ma dame, quant noz maistresses tiennent leur ranc en chambres ou en salles, assises à leur ayse comme noz juges, nous sommes à genoulx devant elles; nous les menons dancer en craincte; nous les servons si diligemment, que nous prevenons leurs demandes; nous semblons estre tant crainctifs de les offenser et tant desirants de les servir, que ceulx qui nous voient ont pitié de nous, et bien souvent nous estiment plus sotz que bestes, transportez d'entendement ou transiz, et donnent la gloire à noz dames, desquelles les contenances sont tant audatieuses et les parolles tant honnestes, qu'elles se font craindre, aymer et estimer de ceulx qui n'en veoient que le dehors. Mais, quant nous sommes à part, où amour seul est juge de noz contenances, nous sçavons très bien qu'elles sont femmes et nous hommes; et à l'heure le nom de *maistresse* est converti en *amye*, et le nom de *serviteur* en *amy*.... Elles ont l'honneur autant que les hommes, qui le leur peuvent donner et oster, ... mais c'est raison aussy que nostre souffrance soit recompensée quand l'honneur ne peult estre blessé.[70]

Saffredent exposes the theory that justifies worldly amours. He urges the ladies to understand and admit this distinction between public and private conduct so that they will not wax indignant, as

[69] Novella 10, disc., p. 83.
[70] *Ibid.*, pp. 83-84.

Floride did, when their obedient suitors suddenly begin to press them closely. He thus confirms Parlamente's fears about the real intentions of so-called romantic lovers, but he also disposes of the vexing question of a woman's honor by insisting that it is equatable with reputation, and that consequently what is not known will not harm her. Lovers may please themselves freely without fear of offending either God or society, provided they abide by the rules of the game.

Saffredent's answer to social disapproval of illicit love touches on the very heart of the *Querelle des femmes* as it appears in the *Heptameron*, for in Marguerite's book the battle is joined around the issue of women's honor. The men, with the exception of Dagoucin and Geburon, repeatedly attribute the ladies' cruelty to false pride and hypocrisy, masked as honor, whereas the ladies insist that true honor consists in clean living, not reputation: it is the lovers who are hypocrites, they contend, masquerading as idealizing Platonists when their intention is really to suborn the conscience of their ladies.[71] What is at issue is the meaning of the term 'honor'; according to Saffredent, it is an invention designed to make women seem better than they are, and all it accomplishes is to stifle the innocence and spontaneity of natural feelings; it perverts the natural order by making virtue – i.e., love – appear sinful.[72] Women are the villains of the piece because, with few exceptions, they will not see that "leur vray honneur gist à monstrer la pudicité du cueur, qui ne doibt vivre que d'amour et non poinct se honorer du vice de dissimullation."[73] It is their vanity and pride which force lovers to dissemble, when they would approach women

[71] E.g. Ennasuitte's statement, Novella 12, disc., pp. 95-96: "Toutesfois, ... si est-ce tousjours la fin de voz oraisons, qui commencent par l'honneur et finissent par le contraire."

[72] "... au commencement que la malice n'estoit trop grande entre les hommes, l'amour y estoit si naifve et forte que nulle dissimullation n'y avoit lieu.... Mais, quant l'avarice et le peché vindrent saisir le cueur et l'honneur, ilz en chasserent dehors Dieu et l'amour; et, en leur lieu, prindrent amour d'eulx-mesmes, hypocrisie et fiction." Novella 42, disc., p. 294.

[73] *Ibid.*, p. 295.

under the impulse of the natural desire to love, the first step towards God. Women are therefore responsible for making of love, that should be beautiful, something terribly complicated and deceitful.[74] But Hircan warns them not to be too sure of themselves; they may claim to be closer to God by reason of their honor, yet actually they are further from salvation than men because they are less honest about their real nature: "Entre nous hommes... sommes plus près de nostre salut, que vous autres, car, ne dissimullans poinct noz fruictz, congnoissons facillement nostre racine; mais, vous qui ne les osez mectre dehors et qui faictes tant de belles œuvres apparantes, à grand peyne congnoistrez-vous ceste racine d'orgueil, qui croist soubz si belle couverture."[75]

The charges levelled against women are as old as the battle of the sexes itself and boil down to the basic accusation that women are far more libidinous than men and that their highly prized virtue is only a monstrous conspiracy intended to earn them a glorious reputation. This view lies behind Hircan's ironic justification of the widow's choice, in the twentieth tale, of her seemingly repulsive stable groom's embraces over those of her highly presentable knightly suitor: "Helas! Madame," he explains to Oisille, "si vous sçaviez la difference qu'il y a d'un gentil homme, qui toute sa vie a porté le harnoys et suivy la guerre, au pris d'un varlet bien nourry sans bouger d'un lieu, vous excuseriez ceste pauvre veuve."[76] Behind the lady stands the whore, a point Simontault makes even more forcefully when he says that women play a double-dealing game, securing both their pleasure and their reputation:

[74] "... celles qui ne povoient avoir en elles ceste honorable amour, disoient que l'honneur le leur deffendoit, et en ont faict une si cruelle loy, que mesmes celles qui ayment parfaictement, dissimullent, estimant vertu estre vice". *Ibid.*, p. 295.
[75] Novella 34, disc., p. 254.
[76] Novella 20, disc., p. 155. Cf. Geburon, Novella 5, disc., p. 37: "Longarine, ... celles qui n'ont poinct accoustumé d'avoir de tels serviteurs que vous, ne tiennent poinct fascheux les Cordeliers; car ilz sont hommes aussy beaulx, aussi fortz et plus reposez que nous autres, qui sommes tous cassez du harnoys."

... il y a des femmes qui veullent avoir des evangelistes pour prescher leur vertu et leur chasteté, et leur font la meilleure chere qu'il leur est possible et la plus privée, les asseurant que, si la conscience et honneur ne les retenoient, elles leur accorderoient leurs desirs. Et les pauvres sotz, quant en quelque compaignye parlent d'elles, jurent qu'ilz mectroient leur doigt au feu sans brusler, pour soustenir qu'elles sont femmes de bien; car ilz ont experimenté leur amour jusques au bout. Ainsi se font louer par les honnestes hommes, celles qui à leurs semblables se montrent telles qu'elles sont, et choisissent ceulx qui ne sçauroient avoir hardiesse de parler; et, s'ilz en parlent, pour leur vile et orde condition, ne seroyent pas creuz.[77]

Even Geburon, who does not as a rule associate himself with his companions' misogyny, agrees that virtue in ladies often comes not from moral principle but as a result of their training and station in life, "en sorte que la vertu des femmes bien nourryes seroit autant appelée coustume que vertu."[78] That a lady's honor is only skin deep fits in with the masculine point of view which prompts Saffredent to declare it is better to love a woman as a woman than to idolize several as if they were sacred images,[79] and, in another context, to assert that one can do a woman whom one desires no greater honor than to take her by force if she is not to be had by persuasion, bribery, or trickery.[80] But Geburon does concede the possibility of a native virtue of the heart, implanted by the spirit of God, and concludes that the honor of women ultimately resides in their chastity, whether they have the honor by virtue of training or of the grace of God. This point of view the ladies champion, all of them insisting, though, that theirs is a code of honor far different from men's because it is based on very different considerations.

The issue is joined when Hircan enunciates his belief that women's so-called honor merely substitutes the vice of pride for the more natural vice of seeking after pleasure, and Nomerfide, expressing regret that so virtuous a wife as Parlamente should be

[77] Novella 20, disc., p. 155.
[78] Novella 5, disc., p. 37.
[79] Novella 12, disc., p. 96.
[80] Novella 18, disc., p. 142.

wasted on one who makes out virtue to be vice, challenges him. The exchange which follows takes us to the heart of the controversy:

> — Je suis bien ayse, dist Hircan, d'avoir une femme qui n'est poinct scandaleuse, comme aussi je ne veulx poinct estre scandaleux; mais, quant à la chasteté de cueur, je croy qu'elle et moy sommes enfans d'Adam et d'Eve; parquoy, en bien nous mirant, n'aurons besoing de couvrir nostre nudité de feuilles, mais plustost confesser nostre fragilité. — Je sçay bien, ce dist Parlamente, que nous avons tous besoing de la grace de Dieu, pour ce que nous sommes tous encloz en peché; si est-ce que noz tentations ne sont pareilles aux vostres, et si nous pechons par orgueil, nul tiers n'en a dommage ny nostre corps et noz mains n'en demeurent souillées. Mais vostre plaisir gist à deshonorer les femmes, et vostre honneur à tuer les hommes en guerre: qui sont deux poincts formellement contraires à la loy de Dieu. — Je vous confesse, ce dist Geburon, ce que vous dictes, mais Dieu qui a dict: "Quiconques regarde par concupiscence est deja adultere en son cueur, et quiconques hayt son prochain est homicide." A vostre advis, les femmes en sont-elles exemptes plus que nous? — Dieu, qui juge le cueur, dist Longarine en donnera sa sentence; mais c'est beaucoup que les hommes ne nous puissent accuser, ... et [Dieu] congnoist si bien la fragilité de noz cueurs, que encores nous aymera-il de ne l'avoir poinct mise à execution.[81]

Hircan and Geburon base their arguments on women's feelings, which they say are no better than men's; Parlamente and Longarine, on the other hand, argue on the basis of women's conduct, which, they say, shows a marked superiority over men's since women do not disobey God's commands. Whatever impulses may lurk in the secret recesses of their hearts as a result of the fallen state of man, they, at least, do not dignify them by founding their honor upon them. Quite to the contrary, their honor, according to Parlamente, is based on something very different — gentleness, patience, and chastity.[82] In other words, where men would let the aggressiveness

[81] Novella 26, disc., pp. 220-221.
[82] "l'honneur des femmes a autre fondement: c'est doulceur, patience et chasteté." Novella 43, disc., p. 301.

of their desires run riot, women stand for a higher morality more likely to insure peace and order in the world. The moral order they represent does not preclude the presence of love – "sans charité et amour," says Parlamente, "ne fault-il pas qu'elles soient";[83] but women must beware the special pleading of courtly lovers, for, strictly speaking, "*mercy* est accorder la grace que l'on demande, et l'on sçait bien celle que les hommes desirent."[84]

The confrontation of masculine and feminine ideals is illuminating for it brings into relief the problem posed by the conflict between the fact of man's emotional and sensual desires and the requirements of Christian morality. Both make strong claims on man's psyche, and the resolution must in some way accommodate them. The first step in Marguerite's proposed solution is to open the eyes of her contemporaries to the idea that the meaning of love is to be found not in a series of amorous adventures but in a stable emotional relationship between two people. "Si l'amour reciprocque," proclaims Parlamente, "ne contente le cueur, tout aultre chose ne le peult contenter."[85] The second step is to place this relationship in marriage – "je ne lairray pas ... desirer que chascun se contantast de son mary, comme je faictz du mien."[86]

Now there is nothing novel in viewing marriage as the institution within which the sexes may properly come together; the principle was formulated for Christianity by St. Paul's famous dictum that for those who cannot contain themselves it is better to marry than to burn (*I Cor.* vii: 9), a dictum which lay at the root of the evangelical writers' theory of marriage as the divinely ordained remedy for those not graced with the gift of continence.[87] Their conception of the Christian marriage involved more than an alternative to fornication, however, and Screech has shown how a liberal interpretation of St. Paul allied to Old Testament views on marriage led to the idea of matrimony as an honorable state endowed with spiritual as well as physical meaning.[88] Within its

---

[83] Novella 56, disc., p. 352.
[84] *Ibid.*, p. 353.
[85] Novella 45, disc., p. 308.

[86] Novella 35, disc., p. 261.
[87] See Screech, pp. 36, 69-71.
[88] Screech, pp. 66-83.

confines a man should, ideally, be able to satisfy his need for companionship and his desire for offspring; it should thus provide him a basis for an orderly life under the guidance of Christian ethics.

Not only did the evangelists combat the traditional theological view which dispraised marriage in favor of celibacy – their main intent, to be sure; they also provided an alternative to the separation between love and marriage effected by the literature of romantic love. The fantasy embodied in the code of courtly love was designed, in part, at least, to compensate for the failure of marriage to provide a satisfactory outlet for the emotional needs of the individual. But if this outlet were to be incorporated into the matrimonial state, there should be no need for the split between a man's emotional and family life. It is no wonder then that the idealistic and profoundly religious Queen of Navarre, deeply disturbed by this split and its consequences in society, should have espoused the evangelical view of the Christian marriage in her treatise of love. For it is nothing less than the revitalization of what had come to be more a social institution than a personal relationship that she proposes in the *Heptameron*, and she would establish within marriage a relationship akin to that sought by her perfect lovers. In this sense hers is a true work of propaganda: she would found her humanism in the mutual love of spouses, just as Rabelais sought to found his in the moral freedom of the individual.[89]

Marguerite's actual discussion of marriage offers nothing revolutionary. Dagoucin formulates – and criticizes – the rationale which determines the selection of a mate. Since marriage is a

[89] Actually, both followed the liberal theology of their day, and Rabelais would generally be on Marguerite's side in the debate on marriage. The significant difference between their attitudes is that Rabelais does not focus exclusively on the emotional relationship marriage entails, and has his hero, Pantagruel, maintain a certain emotional detachment in relation to the marital bond. See Screech, Chapter VII, "The authority of St. Paul, the wisdom of indifference and the *Folly* of the Gospels," pp. 104-125. Also cf.: "Yet in his day there were very few who could envisage marriage, as Margaret of Navarre did in her optimistic moments, as an ideal of greyish whiteness." Screech, p. 131.

social and economic institution, marriages are made to maintain
order and therefore lead more often than not to hell – figuratively
and literally – instead of salvation:

> ... pour entretenir la chose publicque en paix, l'on ne regarde que
> les degrez des maisons, les aages des personnes et les ordonnances
> des loix, sans peser l'amour et les vertuz des hommes, afin de ne
> confondre poinct la monarchye. Et de là vient que les mariages qui
> sont faictz entre pareils, et selon le jugement des parens et des
> hommes, sont bien souvent si differens de cueur, de complexions
> et de conditions, que, en lieu de prendre ung estat pour mener à
> salut, ilz entrent aux faulxbourgs d'enfer.[90]

Geburon disputes the validity of this criticism, reminding Dagoucin that love matches may also end disastrously, just because
reason was thrown to the wind and passion was allowed to determine the marriage choice; for, he explains, "ceste grande amityé
indiscrete tourne souvent à jalousie et en fureur."[91] It is at this
point that Parlamente introduces what is undoubtedly Marguerite's
conception of the ideal marital state: personal desire should match
the dictates of social and economic prudence. Neither private
choice nor social consideration is a praiseworthy foundation for
marriage, says she; what is best is that

> les personnes qui se submectent à la volunté de Dieu ne regardent
> ny à la gloire, ni à l'avarice, ny à la volupté, mais par une amour
> vertueuse et du consentement des parens, desirent de vivre en
> l'estat de mariage, comme Dieu et Nature l'ordonnent. Et com-
> bien que nul estat n'est sans tribulation, si ay-je veu ceulx-là vivre
> sans repentance; et nous ne sommes pas si malheureux en ceste
> compaignie, que nul de tous les mariez ne soyt de ce nombre-là.[92]

In other words, while wisdom and experience dictate that men
and women should adhere to the forms of social convention, what
really matters is the spirit with which one enters matrimony, and
the right spirit means a willing participation in what God and
Nature have ordained as best for man. A marriage so entered into

[90] Novella 40, disc., p. 280.      [91] *Ibid.*, p. 280.      [92] *Ibid.*, p. 280.

is not a perfect state, but it is the best one can hope for. It has the distinct advantage of satisfying man's natural and spiritual needs.

What makes marriage meaningful, then, is its satisfaction of moral and natural requirements; interestingly enough, Hircan shares this view, a view which he defines according to his bias when he explains that there is nothing remarkable about a husband's keeping himself chaste out of love for his wife, since God orders it so, his oath binds him to it, and "Nature qui est soulle, n'est poinct subjecte à tentation ou desir, comme la necessité."[93] But Hircan does distinguish between marital love and "l'amour libre que l'on porte à s'amye,"[94] thus reflecting the mores of the times, illustrated in several tales, whereby a man divides his allegiance between a wife and a courtly mistress. Parlamente, however, allows no such hedging: love belongs *in* marriage rather than outside of it, and while she can praise the husband who turns down a night out with the girls because of his affection for his wife and his love for his Platonic mistress, she holds that "il eust mieulx aymé sa femme, si ce eut esté pour l'amour d'elle seulle."[95] Ideally, then, marriage should satisfy not only the sexual, social, and moral requisites of the partners, but their emotional needs as well.

Parlamente is never very clear about the nature of this conjugal love. Haziness on this subject is due perhaps to Marguerite's awareness that her ideal combination of love and social necessity is rarely found among the aristocracy to whom her book is addressed; when, for instance, Parlamente comes to the end of the definition of a good marriage cited above, Marguerite disposes of her appeal to personal experience by closing the discussion on a note of sadly touching irony: "Hircan, Geburon, Simontault et Saffredent jurerent qu'ilz s'estoient mariez en pareille intention et que jamais ilz ne s'en estoient repentiz *mais quoy qu'il en fust de la verité,* celles à qui il touchoit en furent si contantes, que, ne povans

---

93 Novella 63, disc., pp. 381-382.
94 *Ibid.*, p. 382.
95 *Ibid.*, p. 381. See above, Chapter III. pp. 143-144.

ouyr ung meilleur propos à leur gré, se leverent pour en aller randre graces à Dieu."[96]

Still, despite this touch of pessimism, an outline of Marguerite's conception of a happy marriage emerges from the discussions. One ingredient of a successful marriage must be mutual affection based on respect for the partner's integrity as a person. Thus, when Parlamente comments on Mme. de Loué's infinite patience with her husband's infidelity (Novella 37), she explains why such patience would be impossible for her:

> Quant à moy, il ne me seroit possible d'avoir si longue patience, car, combien que en tous estatz patience soit une belle vertu, j'ay oppinion que en mariage admene enfin inimitié, pour ce que, en souffrant injure de son semable, on est contrainct de s'en separer le plus que l'on peult, et, de ceste estrangeté-là, vient ung despris de la faulte du desloyal; et, en ce despris, peu à peu l'amour diminue, car, d'autant ayme-l'on la chose, que l'on estime la valleur.[97]

Conjugal infidelity is insidious because it corrodes the emotional bonds which link husband and wife, the insult to the partner's feelings making estrangement inevitable. One may imagine that here Marguerite speaks of her own bitter disillusionment, which she voices further when she has Parlamente add that "une femme de bien ne seroit poinct si marrie d'estre battue par collere, que d'estre desprisée pour une qui ne la vault pas";[98] but in any case it is clear that she does not believe love can survive the prolonged humiliation to which extensive philandering subjects a

---

[96] Novella 40, dic., p. 280. The italics are mine.
[97] Novella 37, disc., p. 268. Parlamente's declaration denies Screech's assertion that "for Margaret ... the wise wife affected not to notice her husband's infidelity, and tried to win him back by a sort of aggressive resignation" (Screech, p. 79). Such conduct may be a practical solution, as the 37th tale suggests, but Marguerite would agree with Rabelais' view (Screech, pp. 78-79) that the wife's duty is to mirror the character of her husband, and "if she does not conform to her husband's moral requisites, the fault must lie with himself." Cf. Novella 15, discussed above, Chapter III, pp. 111-112.
[98] Ibid., p. 268.

wife, and she concludes her commentary by saying that the lady in the tale saved her husband from his disreputable love affair out of consideration for their children, and not out of concern for him.

Parlamente's negative comments presuppose the existence of a positive relationship based on mutual trust, and it is evident that she does not restrict the relationship between husband and wife to that of master and obedient servant. She agrees that it is reasonable for the husband to be master in his house, but, she adds, "non pas qu'il nous habandonne ou traicte mal,"[99] and to Oisille's statement, in another discussion, that the wife's duty to her husband is the same as the Church's to Christ – a commonplace of orthodox and evangelical thought – she retorts that this entails an equal responsibility on the husband's part: "Il fauldroit doncques ... que noz mariz fussent envers nous, comme Christ et son Eglise."[100] Thus far, however, her ideas form no more than an abstraction which needs to be translated into concrete terms if the question of what marriage ought to be is to be answered. The impulsive Nomerfide effects the translation when, discussing the clandestine marriage of the fortieth tale, she defends the heroine's action on the ground of the great joy her love-match brought her. The lady, says Nomerfide, had the pleasure of seeing and speaking with one she loved more than herself, and finally "en eut la joissance par mariage, sans scrupule de conscience."[101] Granted it is not the way of the world for a lady of so high rank to marry a suitor of lower rank for love, yet "le plaisir ... est ... d'autant plus grand qu'il a pour son contraire l'oppinion de tous les saiges hommes, et pour son ayde le contentement d'un cueur plain d'amour et le repos de l'ame, veu que Dieu n'y est poinct offensé."[102] In other words, it is *fin amor* which bound the lovers; but their passion, instead of descending to 'mixed' love, sought its consummation in the morally acceptable state of matrimony, thus providing them the

[99] *Ibid.*, p. 269.
[100] Novella 54, disc., p. 344.
[101] Novella 40, disc., p. 277. See above, Chapter III, pp. 115-116.
[102] *Ibid.*, p. 278.

happiness "qui se peult seulle nommer en ce monde *felicité.*"[103] And, she concludes, since the tragic outcome of the tale stems from circumstances external to the love, it in no way detracts from the happiness achieved by the lovers. Nomerfide's defense suggests the idea that when the passionate dream of romantic love is sanctified by the sacrament of marriage, lovers will have found the only true happiness attainable in this world. The 'virtuous love' which, according to Parlamente, finds its fulfillment in wedlock turns out to be none other than romantic love directed to an attainable and morally viable goal.

Attainable and morally viable, the goal is still socially questionable. Nothing illustrates Marguerite's deep-seated conservatism better than Parlamente's unwillingness to endorse Nomerfide's espousal of marriages based on romantic love. True to herself, the Queen's spokesman retains her kinship to the cautiously wise lady of the *Comédie de Mont-de-Marsan* who would have no commerce with the enraptured shepherdess. The choice of a mate, Parlamente feels, is too important a step to be left exclusively to the heart's inclination – a view she expresses when, after the conclusion of the tale, she admonishes the ladies to take its example to heart: "... que nul de vous ayt envye de soy marier, pour son plaisir, sans le consentement de ceulx à qui on doibt porter obeissance; car mariage est ung estat de si longue durée, qu'il ne doibt estre commencé legierement ne sans l'opinion de noz meilleurs amys et parens."[104] Focusing on the lifelong nature of the marital commitment, she urges that reason govern the heart in so serious a matter and emphasizes the need for sympathetic help in making a rational choice. That Marguerite, bred to subjugate her private wishes to political necessity, should distrust undisciplined emotion as a guide to life is not surprising; fully cognizant of the social reality into which man is born, she could not go along with Nomerfide's easy dismissal of the worldly interests which structure so much of man's life. Therefore,

[103] *Ibid.*, p. 278.          [104] *Ibid.*, p. 277.

Parlamente hedges: she wants love in marriage, but she also wants marriages to have the approval custom and mores dictate.[105]

An even stronger case for discipline is made by Oisille, who is dogmatic where Parlamente is hortatory: "si fault-il," she declares, "que nous recongnoissions l'obeissance paternelle, et, par desfault d'icelle, avoir recours aux autres parens."[106] She bases her argument on the immaturity of teen-agers whose free choices will only lead to unhappiness; the wisdom of judicious parents, she feels, is a safer guide than the impulsiveness of youth, and although it might be objected that unhappy love-matches do not necessarily prove the superiority of equally unsatisfactory arranged marriages, Oisille takes a rigorously uncompromising stand against following one's feelings in such matters. Her inflexibility is all the more remarkable in that it comes as part of the discussion of the story of Jacques and Françoise, the two young lovers whose affair leads to a happy marriage[107] – even Longarine, who is usually unbending on matters of morality and decorum, objects only to the premarital seduction, which she finds inexcusable, though she joins in Nomerfide's praise of Jacques for doing the right thing in marrying Françoise. It is the degree of freedom granted the lovers which shocks Oisille, who cannot agree with Saffredent's tolerant view of the case. He, on the other hand, puts his finger on the real issue when, disputing her charge of rape, he contrasts marriages based on love with those based on social and economic considerations. "Est-il meilleur mariage que cestuy-là qui se fait ainsi d'amourettes?" he asks. "C'est pourquoy on dict, en proverbe, que les mariages se font au ciel." But, he continues, "cela ne s'entend pas des mariages forcez, ny qui se font à prix d'argent, et qui sont tenuz pour très approuvez, depuis que le pere et la mere y ont donné consentement."[108] On the one side we have

[105] Marguerite's opposition to clandestine marriages is in line with the attitude of the aristocracy and the Evangelicals of her day. See Screech, pp. 44-54.
[106] Appendix II, disc., pp. 437-438.
[107] Appendix II. See above, Chapter III, pp. 155-157.
[108] Appendix II, disc., p. 437.

the romantic tradition which now says that marriages are made in heaven; on the other, the political view which sees them as social and economic contracts. It is still the age-old conflict between subjective desire and objective social reality that is at issue.

Does Marguerite ever resolve this conflict? Parlamente is strangely non-committal in this discussion, her one contribution being a comment about the mother's simple-mindedness in allowing her daughter to be so easily seduced. We should not, however, look to Parlamente for a final solution; the discussions, after all, define issues far more than they resolve controversies, and the positions on this issue have already been clearly set forth. It is to the stories themselves that we must turn for evidence,[109] and there we find that the one consistent note is that love is a perfectly appropriate foundation for marriage, provided that the match does not violate important tenets of social propriety. Where a real breach of the social code does occur, the results can be only unhappy: Rolandine's secret marriage, unconsummated because she obviously accepts the rules which disapprove of clandestine unions, is an empty shell, while her aunt's equally secret marriage is brought to a tragic end because of the deliberate violation of these same rules. But in the case of Jacques and Françoise, the emotional choice is also socially reasonable, and theirs is a successful union. It may be true that the happy ending is due to the fact that this story expresses the values of middle-class life, and therefore belongs to the so-called realistic tradition, whereas the tragic endings of the other two tales derive from the conventions of courtly literature, but Marguerite has clearly announced that her tales are not to be viewed as manifestations of literary convention. They are to be taken as true, and if they are, Jacques and Françoise present what is without doubt the happiest reconciliation of all those aspects any view of marriage must consider.

Marguerite's considered conclusion seems to be, then, that

[109] The three novellas concerned with love matches are the stories of Rolandine, of her aunt, and of the young Parisian lovers, nos. 21, 40, and Appendix II. See above, Chapter III, pp. 113-118.

marriage is still the best human arrangement available wherein the contradictory requirements of man's erotic and social nature may be reasonably satisfied. If it is going to fulfill this promise, however, it must be rooted in love, the universal bond, and keep faith with Christian ethics. Wedlock is not a perfect state and holds its share of tribulation, as Parlamente realizes; it is nonetheless the best chance man has for true happiness in this world.

# CHAPTER V / CONCLUSION

Sister of a king, Marguerite de Navarre was a princess of the world who, although enjoying her brilliant career at court, was not content with the superficial rewards of worldly success; possessed of a generous heart and trained from earliest childhood to give of herself, she experienced an emotional void which her active participation in the affairs of the kingdom could not fill. In her search for durable values she discovered the spiritual message of the Gospels and sought fulfillment in the plenitude of God's love. She did not, for all that, renounce the world: neither her own lively interest in it nor her sense of duty to the crown would have allowed it. But the Evangelists who opened her eyes to the spirit of the Bible provided her with an ideal which was to remain the guiding principle of her spiritual life to the end of her days: a Christian humanism which envisioned a world attuned to God's word as revealed in the Holy Scriptures.

Marguerite's writings are the record of her search for meaning in the transitory phenomenon that is life. Athirst for the absolute, she was unwilling to relinquish the concrete reality of existence, and since Christian humanism and Neoplatonism provided her with systems of thought designed to resolve the seeming dichotomy between earthly and heavenly life, she embraced them enthusiastically. But she still had to make her own peace with the contradictory claims of the secular and spiritual values which called for her allegiance. She found no shortcut leading directly to God; man's path, she felt, lay through the world, where, supported by faith and guided by an enlightened understanding of the Bible, he could hope, with God's grace, to make his way to heaven.

Divine grace was a gift of love, and Marguerite pinned her hopes on love. With the Neoplatonists, she believed that love is the universal bond which unites Creation and links it to the Creator. But she also knew that in its manifestation as human passion it can be a disruptive force. In the *Heptameron* she sought to clarify the nature of love and to show that its destructive action is due to the anarchic violence of appetitive drives uncontrolled by the moral will. An intense feminist, she attributed this anarchy to masculine aggressiveness and pride, and went so far as to deny concupiscent women the right to call themselves women. And in opposition to the adulterous system of courtly love she propounded the ideal of the Christian marriage, within which natural appetite could be harmonized with Christian ethics.

Although Marguerite's inquiry into the nature and ways of love had a serious purpose, she only hinted at the direction she wished to see human affection and desire take. To have done more would have destroyed the wonderful balance between realism and idealism by means of which this remarkable Queen was able to encompass the multifarious nature of human experience. Her book is not a formal treatise which undertakes to package questions and answers, problems and solutions, in neatly ordered fashion, with all loose ends carefully tucked in. It is a discussion which illuminates without claiming to reach absolutely final conclusions. Man's situation is kept plainly in sight, and his ultimate goal is discerned as never more than a possibility in this world; the path leading through reality to an ideal remains to be discovered by every man through the trial-and-error process of living. At the core of the book lies what gives it its unique quality – Marguerite's imaginative vision of this process. Imitating the progression of life itself, the *Heptameron* finds in the midst of its inconclusiveness and contradictions tentative resting points from which the human scene may be surveyed with sympathetic understanding.

In the last analysis, the *Heptameron* defies classification. It is part of a well-worn tradition that began with the love poetry of the troubadours. The ideas it draws from this tradition – a tradition comprising the love lyric, the romance, and the Neoplatonist discourse – speak through the 'realist' narrative tradition of the novella. Lacking the imaginative force to create a myth, Marguerite could achieve no synthesis comparable to Dante's; never the detached artist Boccaccio was, she could write no *Decameron* either. Hers is undoubtedly a minor work, but nonetheless a classic, for despite its imitative features it bears the stamp of an individualized sensibility which, by imposing a unified style on its material, recreates, however modestly, the world. It also, discreetly, points to the future: the observation of character in relation to passion and *milieu* foreshadows the dominant interest of seventeenth-century classicism, and the seemingly disconnected, contradictory discursiveness of its discussions anchored in the idiosyncratic nature of the human personality leads to Montaigne.[1] The *Heptameron*, standing as it were mid-way between the neo-classical and individualistic tendencies of the Renaissance, makes its valid, original, and entertaining contribution to culture. Like all classics, it tries to civilize the human animal.

[1] Cf. the following observation: "En réalité, *l'Heptaméron* est autre chose qu'une série d'anecdotes suivies de commentaires. Il pourrait être considéré, en se plaçant uniquement au point de vue de la charpente, comme les premiers 'essais' de notre littérature concernant les relations entre les deux sexes." Telle, p. 96.

# SELECTED BIBLIOGRAPHY

Andreas Capellanus. *The Art of Courtly Love*, J. J. Parry, trans. and ed. New York: Columbia University Press, 1941.

Boccaccio, Giovanni. *Amorosa Visione*, in *Opere Volgare di Giovanni Boccaccio*, XIV. Firenze: Moutier, 1833.

— *Decameron. Filocolo. Ameto. Fiammetta*, a cura di E. Bianchi, C. Salinari, N. Sapegno (La Letteratura Italiana, Storia e Testi, vol. 8). Milano-Napoli: Riccardo Ricciardi, n. d.

— *Il Filostrato*, in *Opere Volgare di Giovanni Boccaccio*, XIII. Firenze: Moutier, 1831.

Castiglione, Baldassare. *Il Libro del Cortegiano*, in *Opere di Baldassare Castiglione, Giovanni della Casa, Benvenuto Cellini*, a cura di Carlo Cordié (La Letteratura Italiana, Storia e Testi, vol. 27). Milano-Napoli: Riccardo Ricciardi, n. d.

Crane, Thomas F. *Italian Social Customs of the Sixteenth Century and their Influence on the Literature of Europe*. New Haven: Yale University Press, 1920.

De Sanctis, Francesco. *History of Italian Literature*, Joan Redfern, trans. 2 vols. New York: Basic Books, n. d.

Ely, Gladys. "The Limits of Realism in the *Heptaméron* of Marguerite de Navarre," *Romanic Review*, XLIII, No. 1 (Feb. 1952) 3-11.

Febvre, Lucien. *Autour de l'Heptaméron: amour sacré, amour profane*. Paris: Gallimard, 1944.

— *Le Problème de l'incroyance au XVIe siècle. La religion de Rabelais*. Paris: Albin Michel, 1942.

Ficino, Marsilio. *In Convivium Platonis De Amore Commentarius*, in *Marsile Ficin, Commentaire sur le Banquet de Platon*, Raymond Marcel, trans. and ed. Paris: Société d'Edition "Les Belles Lettres," 1956.

Héroet, Antoine. *Oeuvres poétiques*, Ferdinand Gohin, ed. Paris: Hachette, 1909.

Huizinga, Johan. *Erasmus and the Age of Reformation*. New York: Harper and Row, 1957.

Jeanroy, Alfred. *La Poésie lyrique des troubadours*. 2 vols. Toulouse, Paris: Privat, Didier, 1934.

Jourda, Pierre. "L'Heptaméron, livre pré-classique," in *Studi in onore di Carlo Pellegrini* (Biblioteca di Studi Francesi, 2) pp. 133-136. Torino: Società Editrice Internazionale, 1963.

— *Marguerite d'Angoulême, Duchesse d'Alençon, Reine de Navarre (1492-1549), étude biographique et littéraire*. 2 vols. Paris: Champion, 1930.

— *Répertoire analytique et chronologique de la correspondance de Marguerite d'Angou-*

lême, *Duchesse d'Alençon, Reine de Navarre (1492-1549)*. Paris: Champion, 1930.

*La Chastelaine de Vergi*, in *Poètes et romanciers du Moyen-Age*, Albert Pauphilet, ed. Paris: Bibliothèque de la Pléiade, 1952.

La Ferrière-Percy, Comte H. de. *Marguerite d'Angoulême, son livre de dépenses (1540-1549)*. Paris: Aubry, 1862.

Lebègue, Raymond. "La femme qui mutile son visage (*Heptaméron X*)," *Comptes-rendus des séances de l'année 1959*, Académie des inscriptions et belles-lettres, Paris (Avril-Décembre) 176-184.

Lefranc, Abel. "Marguerite de Navarre et le platonisme de la Renaissance," in *Grands écrivains français de la Renaissance*. Paris: Champion, 1914.

— "Le platonisme et la littérature en France," in *Grands écrivains français de la Renaissance*. Paris: Champion, 1914.

Marguerite de Navarre. *Les Dernières poésies de Marguerite de Navarre*, Abel Lefranc, ed. Paris: Armand Colin, 1896.

— *L'Heptaméron*, Michel François ed. Nouvelle édition revue et corrigée. Paris: Garnier, n. d.

— *Lettres de Marguerite d'Angoulême*, F. Génin, ed. Paris: Jules Renouard, 1841.

— *Les Marguerites de la Marguerite des princesses*, F. Frank, ed. 4 vols. Paris: Librairie des Bibliophiles, 1873.

— *Nouvelles lettres de Marguerite d'Angoulême*, F. Génin, ed. Paris: Jules Renouard, 1842.

— *Théâtre profane*, Verdun L. Saulnier, ed. Paris: Droz, 1958.

Mayer, C.-A. *La Religion de Marot*. Genève: Droz, 1960.

Mignon, M. *Les Affinités intellectuelles de l'Italie et de la France*. Paris: Hachette, 1923.

Montaigne, Michel de. *Essais*, Albert Thibaudet, ed. Paris: Bibliothèque de la Pléiade, 1950.

Nelson, John Charles. *Renaissance Theory of Love*. New York: Columbia University Press, 1958.

Petrarca, Francesco. *Petrarch, The First Modern Scholar and Man of Letters*, J. H. Robinson and H. W. Rolfe, trans. and eds. New York and London: G. P. Putnam's Sons, 1898.

— *Prose*, a cura di G. Martellotti, P. G. Ricci, E. Carrara, E. Bianchi (La Letteratura Italiana, Storia e Testi, vol. 7). Milano-Napoli: Riccardo Ricciardi, n. d.

— *Rime, Trionfi, e Poesie Latine*, a cura di F. Neri, G. Martellotti, E. Bianchi, N. Sapegno (La Letteratura Italiana, Storia e Testi, vol. 6). Milano-Napoli: Riccardo Ricciardi, n. d.

Picot, E. *Les Français italianisants au XVIe siècle*. 2 vols. Paris: Champion, 1906.

Renaudet, A. "Marguerite de Navarre, à propos d'un ouvrage récent," *Revue du XVIe Siècle*, XVIII (1931) 272-308.

—       *Préréforme et humanisme à Paris pendant les premières guerres d'Italie (1494-1517)*. 2e éd. revue et corrigée. Paris: Librairie d'Argences, 1953.

Robb, Nesca A. *Neoplatonism of the Italian Renaissance*. London: Allen and Unwin, 1935.

Rougemont, Denis de. *Love in the Western World*, rev. and augm. ed. Garden City: Anchor Books, 1957.

Rudel, Jaufré. *Les Chansons de Jaufré Rudel*, Alfred Jeanroy ed. Paris: Champion, 1915.

Saulnier, Verdun L. "Marguerite de Navarre: art médiéval et pensée nouvelle," *Revue Universitaire*, 63e année (1954) 154-162.

Screech, M. A. *The Rabelaisian Marriage*. London: Edward Arnold, 1958.

Symonds, J. A. *Renaissance in Italy: Italian Literature*. 2 vols. New York: Holt, 1885.

Telle, Emile V. *L'Oeuvre de Marguerite d'Angoulême, Reine de Navarre, et la Querelle des Femmes*. Toulouse: Privat, 1937.

Valency, Maurice. *In Praise of Love, an Introduction to the Love-Poetry of the Renaissance*. New York: Macmillan, 1958.

Vernay, Henri. *Les divers sens du mot raison autour de l'œuvre de Marguerite d'Angoulême, Reine de Navarre (1492-1549)* (Studia Romanica, vol. 3). Heidelberg: C. Winter, Universitätsverlag, 1962.

Westermarck, Edward. *The History of Human Marriage*. 3 vols. 5th ed. New York: Allerton, 1922.

# REPRINTS FROM OUR COMPARATIVE LITERATURE STUDIES

## Through the University of North Carolina Press
### Chapel Hill, North Carolina

2. Werner P. Friederich. DANTE'S FAME ABROAD, 1350-1850. The influence of Dante Alighieri on the Poets and Scholars of Spain, France, England, Germany, Switzerland and the United States. Rome, 1950 and 1966. Pp. 584. Paper, $ 10.00.

10. Charles E. Passage. DOSTOEVSKI THE ADAPTER. A Study in Dostoevski's Use of the Tales of Hoffmann. 1954. Reprinted 1963. Pp. x, 205. Paper, $ 3.50. Cloth, $ 4.50.

11. Werner P. Friederich and David H. Malone. OUTLINE OF COMPARATIVE LITERATURE. From Dante Alighieri to Eugene O'Neill. 1954. Third Printing, 1962. Pp. 460. Cloth, $ 6.50.

## Through Russell & Russell, Inc.
### Publishers, 156 Fifth Avenue
### New York, N. Y. 10010

1. Fernand Baldensperger and Werner P. Friederich. BIBLIOGRAPHY OF COMPARATIVE LITERATURE. 1950. 729 p. Cloth, $ 15.00.

6, 7, 9, 14, 16, 18, 21, 25 and 27. W. P. Friederich & H. Frenz (eds): YEARBOOKS OF COMPARATIVE AND GENERAL LITERATURE. Vols. I (1952) to IX (1960). Cloth, $ 6.50 per volume.

## Through Johnson Reprint Corporation
### 111 Fifth Avenue
### New York, N. Y. 10003

4. GOETHE'S SORROWS OF YOUNG WERTER, TRANSLATED BY GEORGE TICKNOR. Edited with Introduction and Critical Analysis by Frank G. Ryder. Cloth, $ 8.00.

5. Helmut A. Hatzfeld. A CRITICAL BIBLIOGRAPHY OF THE NEW STYLISTICS APPLIED TO THE ROMANCE LITERATURES, 1900-1952. Cloth, $ 12.00.

26. DANTE'S LA VITA NUOVA, TRANSLATED BY RALPH WALDO EMERSON. Edited and annotated by J. Chesley Mathews. Cloth, $ 8.00.

28. Haskell M. Block (ed.) THE TEACHING OF WORLD LITERATURE. Cloth, $ 6.00.

30. Oskar Seidlin. ESSAYS IN GERMAN AND COMPARATIVE LITERATURE. Cloth, $ 10.00.